GETTING STARTED WITH GERMAN

Beginning German for Homeschoolers and Self-Taught Students of Any Age

WILLIAM E. LINNEY

BRANDON SIMPSON

ARMFIELD ACADEMIC PRESS

In memoriam Dr. Thomas Leech, Professor of German

Published by Armfield Academic Press

Chief editorial consultant: Elisabeth Stratmann

Editorial consultants: Rogelio Garza, Lisa Rösch, Michael D. Sweet

Editorial assistants: Benjamin R. Turnbull, Katherine L. Bradshaw

ISBN: 978-1-62611-011-3

CONTENTS

PREFACE

My first book, *Getting Started with Latin*, was a labor of love. I wrote it to help homeschooled and self-taught students learn beginning Latin at home, without a teacher. Since the publication of *Getting Started with Latin*, the response has been positive (except for that one nasty email I got a few years back). People seem to like the one-thing-at-a-time format of the book, which never leaves them lost and wondering what just happened like other books do. This is significant because homeschooled and self-taught students are a special group of people who need specialized materials—products that allow them to learn at home without access to a teacher who specializes in that particular subject.

After *Getting Started with Latin*, my friend Antonio Orta and I wondered if we could apply that same one-thing-at-a-time approach to a modern language such as Spanish, and so *Getting Started with Spanish* was born. Then, a few years later, Brandon Simpson and I wrote *Getting started with French*. Now Brandon and I bring you this second collaboration, *Getting Started with German*.

Like every book in the series, *Getting Started with German* is designed to accomplish several educational goals. I have designed this book to…

- Be self-explanatory, self-paced, self-contained and inexpensive
- Allow the student to make progress with or without a teacher
- Provide plenty of practice exercises after each new concept so that the student can master each idea before moving on to the next one
- Provide audio recordings for aural practice and supplementary instruction
- Avoid making German any more difficult than it actually is

Getting Started with German was created to meet the unique needs of homeschooled and self-taught students. It is self-contained, with no extra materials to purchase (such as pronunciation recordings, answer keys, or teachers' editions). It's also in a large format to make it easier to use, and non-consumable so it can be used with multiple children. The answer key is in the back of the book, and there are free pronunciation recordings and author's commentary recordings available at the following website:

www.GettingStartedWithGerman.com

In this book, new words and concepts are introduced in a gradual yet systematic fashion. Each lesson provides many exercises for practicing the new material while reviewing material from previous lessons.

Getting Started with German makes German accessible to students of any age or educational background. Because this book moves so gradually, you probably will not say *This is too hard for me. I quit!* Instead, these bite-size lessons leave you encouraged and ready to continue. But when you do finish this book, don't let your German studies end there. Learning and using a foreign language is quite a thrill—so keep going, and above all, have fun with it!

William E. Linney

HOW TO USE THIS BOOK

This book is structured around one main teaching method: Teach one concept at a time and let the student master that concept before introducing the next one. With that in mind, read the tips listed below to help you use this book to the greatest advantage.

THE NEW WORD

Start each lesson by observing the new word for that particular lesson. All German words in this book are in **bold print** so they will be easy to recognize. The meaning of the new word is in *italics*. In some lessons you will learn a new concept and in others you will simply review material from previous lessons.

PRONUNCIATION

The best way to learn correct pronunciation is by listening and copying what you hear. Visit www.GettingStartedWithGerman.com to hear the free pronunciation recordings. In these recordings, each new word and exercise is read aloud so you can not only read but hear the exercises. These free audio recordings will help you achieve proper pronunciation and provide you with lots of opportunities for aural translation practice.

If needed, there will be a written pronunciation tip at the beginning of a particular lesson. These tips are there to give you a general idea of how the word sounds and to help you avoid the most likely pronunciation errors. To further assist you in achieving proper pronunciation, there is a pronunciation guide at the end of the book.

GRAMMATICAL INFORMATION

If needed, a lesson may contain an explanation of how to use the new word introduced in that lesson. Charts and examples are used to give the reader a clear presentation of the grammar knowledge needed for that particular lesson.

The book's website has special audio commentary recordings which have been prepared by the author. These recordings discuss each lesson, so if you have any trouble understanding the material presented in a lesson, you will have plenty of help on hand.

THE EXERCISES

Armed with the knowledge of the new word and how to use it, begin to translate the exercises. In a homeschool environment, it is probably best to have students write their answers in a notebook. Older students and adults may prefer to do the exercises mentally. Next, turn to the answer key in the back of the book to see if your translations are correct. By comparing the German and the English, you will learn from your mistakes. Translating the exercises over and over (even memorizing them) will enhance learning and speed your progress. After you have translated the exercises and you know what they mean, listen to the audio recordings over and over for practice. The more you listen, the faster your progress will be.

REPEATED LISTENING

After you have studied the exercises and you know what they mean, you are in a position to use an extremely effective language learning technique. This technique involves reading or hearing understandable material in the foreign language that you are studying. If you are studying a foreign language, and you hear or read lots of material that you can't understand, it doesn't really do you any good. But if you hear or read something that is at your current level of learning, you are getting some good practice interpreting that language because the material is understandable.

Here's how this applies to you: once you have studied the exercises for a certain lesson, and you know what the exercises mean, you should listen to the audio recordings for that lesson over and over. Don't just listen once or twice—listen to them a hundred times, until everything you hear sounds natural to you. Listen in the car, while cleaning up, etc. This study method will help your brain to process, absorb, and get used to the language.

PRACTICING CONVERSATIONAL SKILLS

Now comes the really important part. Once you understand the exercises, it's time to practice using what you have learned. The ideal situation would be to have a family member or friend with whom you can practice speaking German on a daily basis. Repetition is the key here. Try repeating the exercises over and over to each other or making up your own similar sentences. We have tried to make the vocabulary in this book pertain to common everyday activities so that you can take what you learn here and immediately begin to use it in actual conversations.

If you can't practice with a friend or family member, you can still accomplish a lot by practicing with the pronunciation recordings. You can practice your pronunciation skills by trying to pronounce the exercises just like the speaker. Or, you can practice your listening skills by repeatedly listening to and interpreting the recordings.

GERMAN COMPOSITION

For an additional challenge, you can try to translate the answers in the answer key back into German using the knowledge you have gained from that lesson. This is called German composition. Figuring out how to write something in German can be a great learning tool because it requires you to think about the material in a different way. Try it and see! Again, it is probably best to write these exercises in a notebook.

DON'T PUT THE CART BEFORE THE HORSE

Do not skip ahead to a future lesson. Because each lesson builds directly on the preceding lessons, do the lessons in the order given. If you start to feel lost or confused, back up a few lessons and review. Or, take a break and come back to the material at a later time. Remember that review and repetition are essential when learning any language. One of the best things you can do to improve your understanding of German is to review the lessons repeatedly.

STAY FLEXIBLE

Everyone has a different learning style, so use this book in ways that fit your needs or the needs of your students. You can learn German as a family, on your own, or in a homeschool environment. Be creative! You could even have one night of the week when the entire family is only allowed to speak German. Who knows? You may think of a way to use this book that no one else has thought of (putting it under the short leg of the kitchen table does not count).

TESTS AND QUIZZES

To give a student a test or quiz, simply back up to a previous lesson and have the student translate those exercises without looking at the answers. Then, the teacher or parent can grade the exercises using the answers in the back of the book. Another possibility would be to test the student's listening skills by having him or her translate the exercises directly from the audio recording for that lesson.

SCHEDULING

Some homeschool parents like a lot of structure in their teaching schedules, while others prefer a less structured learning environment. Depending on your personal preferences, you may either plan to cover a certain number of lessons in a certain period of time, or allow your students to determine their own pace. It's up to you.

HOW MUCH TIME PER DAY?

A few minutes a day with this book is better than longer, less frequent sessions. Thirty minutes a day is ideal for language study. Of course, this may vary with each student's age, ability, and interest level.

SELF-TAUGHT ADULTS

Adults who use this book will enjoy the freedom of learning German whenever and wherever they please. High school and college students may use it to get a head start before taking a German class, to satisfy curiosity, or to try something new. Busy adults may use it to study at lunchtime, break time, or while commuting to work (as long as someone else is driving the vehicle). The short lessons in this book will fit any schedule.

SURF THE NET!

Don't forget about the website that accompanies this book. Here's that web address again, in case you missed it:

www.GettingStartedWithGerman.com

It has free resources to aid you in your study of German. Be sure to check it out!

LESSON ONE

THE COMMON ROOTS OF ENGLISH AND GERMAN

For English speakers, German is an interesting language to study because of the connection between English and German. The reason for this connection is that both languages share a common ancestor. If you think of all the languages of the world as a family tree, English and German are from the same branch of the tree. In the 5th century A.D., Germanic tribes came to Great Britain from the areas that make up northern Germany and Denmark today. These tribes, called the Angles, Saxons, and Jutes (pronounced *yoots*) settled in what is today England. In fact, the word *England* is really *Angle-land*…the land of the Angles.

So as you study German, you will find many similarities between the two languages both in structure and in vocabulary. If you see something in German that reminds you of English, it's not your imagination—it's because the two languages are distant cousins.

LESSON TWO

PRONUNCIATION

From the perspective of an English speaker, German words usually don't sound the way they are spelled. Let's examine some of the specific ways that German pronunciation differs from what you would expect as an English speaker.

For starters, when the letter *d* comes at the end of a German word, it sounds like a *t*. Here's an example:

Hund

The word **Hund** means *dog* (it's related to our English word *hound*). When you pronounce it, pronounce it like *hoont*.

By the way, all nouns in German are capitalized. That's why the word **Hund** has a capital *h* at the beginning.

In German, the letter *s* can make several different sounds depending on its position in a word. Here's one common thing you will see in this book: the letter *s* making a *z* sound:

Sohn

The word **Sohn** means *son*. Since the *s* sounds like a *z* in this word, **Sohn** sounds like something like *zone*.

In German, the letter *v* doesn't sound like the *v* in *vest*—it sounds like the *f* in *fish*. Here's an example:

Vater

So the word **Vater**, which means *father*, sounds something like *FAH-tuh* (more about the *r* sound later).

The letter combination *ch* can sound different ways depending on the kind of vowel sound that comes before it. Here are a couple of words in which *ch* sounds like the air rushing over the top of your tongue, like when you start to say words such as *huge* or *human*.

- **ich**
- **durch**

Some of you may live in parts of the U.S. where the letter *h* is not pronounced at the beginning of *huge* or *human*. You might pronounce those words as *yuge* or *youman*. If this applies to you, take a few minutes to practice making this initial *h* sound so you can apply it to the pronunciation of certain German words.

After strong vowels like *a*, *o*, and *u*, the *ch* letter combination has a scraping sound at the roof of the mouth, as in these words:

- **noch**
- **Buch**

2

The *ch* combination can also sound like a *k* in certain situations. For example, *ch* can sound like a *k* when it comes at the beginning of a word, as seen in the word **Charakter** which means *character*. Also, *ch* can sound like a *k* when it is followed by an *s*, as seen in the word **wachsen**, which means *to grow.*

In this lesson, we haven't covered every difference between German pronunciation and English pronunciation, but we have at least covered the major ones so you can get started. Of course, we will encounter more of them, and we will point them out to you when we see them.

Be sure to visit www.GettingStartedWithGerman.com to hear the free pronunciation recordings. In these free audio recordings, each new word and exercise is read aloud by a native speaker so you can hear and copy a real, authentic pronunciation.

LESSON THREE

GENDER

In German, each noun is either masculine, feminine, or neuter. This quality that nouns have is called *gender*. This concept is easy to understand with people and animals—after all, we know that animals and people are either male or female. But in German, even words for non-living things have gender. For instance, pencils, cars, and houses all have gender in the German language.

When it comes to the gender of nouns, there are two kinds of gender to think about: natural gender and grammatical gender. According to natural gender, the word for *man* ought to be masculine, and the word for *woman* ought to be feminine. And most of the time, this is the case. But words aren't real life—words are just sounds and representations of meaning that help us communicate ideas and thoughts about real life.

Sometimes, the grammatical gender of a noun can be different from what its natural gender ought to be. For example, the German word **Mädchen** which means *girl* is grammatically neuter, even though the natural gender of a girl is feminine. I'm always amused by the fact that in Latin, the noun **virtus**, which means *manliness*, is grammatically feminine!

3

So for you, as a beginning German student, what this means is that whenever you learn a German noun, you need to remember the gender of that particular word—that is, whether it is masculine, feminine, or neuter.

LESSON FOUR

ARTICLES

Articles are words such as *the, a,* and *an.* Let's take a look at some examples:

- <u>The</u> man
- <u>The</u> woman
- <u>A</u> chair
- <u>An</u> apple

A noun is a person, place or thing. In each of the examples above, we used an article to introduce each noun.

What is the difference between *a* and *an*? Please look at the following examples:

- A book
- An apple

A and *an* are actually the same word but with one important difference: *a* comes before a noun that starts with a consonant and *an* comes before a noun that starts with a vowel. Why the variation in spelling? This is done in order to make pronunciation easier. For example, it is easier to say *a book* than *an book.* Likewise, it is easier to say *an apple* than *a apple.* So try to think of *a* and *an* as two variations of the same word.

In the next few lessons, we will learn how to use articles in German.

LESSON FIVE

THE LETTER R

Take a moment to think about how you pronounce the letter *r*. When your mouth and tongue make an *r* sound, what movements do they make? Let's try a little experiment together: say the word *red* slowly and try to notice the movements you make inside your mouth as you pronounce the initial *r* sound. Do that now before you continue reading.

Most likely, what you are doing is raising your tongue upward and toward the rear of your mouth, partially closing off the flow of air. For some reason, positioning your tongue in this manner makes the *urr* kind of *r* sound that starts out the word *red*. This is an important concept, so if you don't understand it, keep experimenting with it until you understand what is going on.

Now that you understand how you usually pronounce an *r* sound in English, we have an important message for you: in German, the letter *r* is not pronounced this way. You have to learn how to pronounce two new kinds of *r* sounds so you can pronounce the German language correctly. Here they "r."

1. An *r* at the beginning of a syllable
2. An *r* at the end of a syllable

AT THE BEGINNING OF A SYLLABLE

The kind of *r* sound that comes at the beginning of a syllable is produced by lifting the back of your tongue and making a gargling sound in your throat. Practice this sound by saying the German word **rot** which means *red*:

rot

For those of you who have already studied French, this sound will be easy because it is the same *r* sound found in French. But it's not the same as the rolled *r* sound in Spanish (so don't do that).

AT THE END OF A SYLLABLE

This kind of *r* sound isn't really an *r* at all—when the letter *r* comes at the end of a syllable, it doesn't really make any kind of sound. Instead, you just leave

5

your mouth open and say the accompanying vowel sound. That's why we call this sound an *open r* sound. Let's use the German word for *father* as an example.

Vater

This word sounds something like *FAH-tuh*, with an open *uh* kind of sound at the end. You should *not* raise the back of your tongue and make an *urrr* sound like *FAH-turrr*.

Here's another example: notice that in the word *Arnold*, the first syllable is comprised of the *a* and the *r*.

Arnold

Therefore the *r* comes at the end of that first syllable. For this reason, the *r* sound there will be an open *r* sound, and the word will sound something like *AAAH-nold*.

Take a few minutes to experiment with these sounds until you get used to them—and when you do, you'll be on your way toward authentic German pronunciation!

LESSON SIX

NEW WORD   **der**

MEANING   *the*

PRONUNCIATION TIP: The *r* in **der** comes at the end of a syllable, so it will have an open *r* sound. **Der** sounds something like *DAY-uh* (don't pronounce it like *dare* or *durr*).

In lesson 3, we learned that German nouns are either masculine, feminine, or neuter. In German, articles (words like *the*, *a*, or *an*) are also either masculine, feminine, or neuter. So if you have a masculine noun, and you want to introduce it with *a* or *an*, you must use a masculine article. Likewise, if you want to introduce a feminine noun, you must use a feminine article.

Der, our new word for this lesson, is the masculine form of the word *the.* In the next lesson, we will use **der** to introduce a masculine German noun.

LESSON SEVEN

NEW WORD   **Mann**

MEANING   *man*

PRONUNCIATION TIP: The vowel sound in **Mann** sounds like the *a* in *father*.

Mann is our first German noun. It is masculine, so if you want to put the article *the* in front of it, you must use the masculine form, which is **der**.

From this point forward, we will give you some exercises in each lesson. See if you can translate the exercises below correctly. The answers are in the back of the book in case you need to peek.

Quick reminder: In German, all nouns are capitalized, no matter where they are in a sentence.

EXERCISES

1. **Mann**
2. **Der Mann**

And don't forget to listen to the pronunciation recordings, too, so you can hear how the exercises sound.

The answers to this lesson are on page 189.

LESSON EIGHT

NEW WORD   **die**

MEANING   *the*

PRONUNCIATION TIP: **Die** sounds like *dee*, not like the English word *die*.

You already know that **der** is the masculine form of *the*. Now it is time to learn the feminine form.

Die, our new word for this lesson, is the feminine form of the article *the*. In the next lesson, we will use **die** to introduce a feminine German noun.

LESSON NINE

NEW WORD   **Frau**

MEANING   *woman*

PRONUNCIATION TIP: **Frau** sounds something like the English word *frown*, but without the *n* at the end. The *r* in *Frau* comes at the beginning of the syllable (combined with the *f*) so it gets the gargling *r* sound in the back of the mouth.

Frau is our first feminine German noun. Since it is feminine, if you want to put *the* in front of it, you must use the feminine form, which is **die**.

Remember that all German nouns are capitalized, no matter where they are in a sentence.

EXERCISES

1. **Frau**
2. **Die Frau**
3. **Mann**
4. **Der Mann**

Answers on page 189.

LESSON TEN

NEW WORD   **das**

MEANING   *the*

PRONUNCIATION TIP: The *a* in **das** sounds like the *a* in *father*.

You already know that **der** is the masculine form of *the* and that **die** is the feminine form of *the*. Now, it is time to learn the neuter form.

Das, our new word for this lesson, is the neuter form of the article *the*. Examine the following chart:

MASCULINE	FEMININE	NEUTER
der	**die**	**das**

Soon we will use **das** to introduce a neuter German noun.

A NOTE ABOUT MEMORIZATION

A few lessons ago we told you that it is important for you to remember the gender of each new noun that you learn. And one good way to do that is to memorize a noun and its article together. Let's say, for example, that you want to memorize the word **Mann**. If you say it over and over to memorize it, don't just say **Mann** over and over—instead, say **der Mann**. That way, you are memorizing the article along with the noun, helping yourself to remember the noun's gender. Go ahead and get into this habit now while you are still a beginner, and it will pay big dividends down the road.

LESSON ELEVEN

THE UMLAUT

An **Umlaut** (pronounced *OOM-lout*) is a marking that consists of two dots that sit above a vowel, like this:

ä

An **Umlaut** indicates a change in pronunciation for certain vowels. For example, the letter *a* without the **Umlaut** sounds like the *a* in *father*, but with the **Umlaut** over it, it sounds something like the *e* in *let*, *met*, or *bet*.

The **Umlaut** has a long history. Long ago, as the German language developed, the pronunciation of certain vowels began to change. German writers wrote an additional *e* after a vowel to indicate a pronunciation change. Later, this extra *e* was written as a small *e* above another vowel. Then they began to write the *e* as two small dots, and that's how the modern **Umlaut** was born.

In the next lesson, you'll learn your first word with an **Umlaut** in it.

LESSON TWELVE

NEW WORD   **Mädchen**

MEANING   *girl*

PRONUNCIATION TIP: Notice that the *a* in **Mädchen** has an **Umlaut** over it, so it will sound something like the *e* in *let* or *met*. The *ch* in the middle of **Mädchen** sounds like the whooshing sound at the beginning of the word *huge*. Don't pronounce the *-chen* in **Mädchen** like the English word *chin*—it doesn't sound like that.

Mädchen, our new word for this lesson, means *girl*. Remember what we told you about natural gender and grammatical gender? Even though a girl is feminine according to natural gender, the word **Mädchen** is grammatically neuter because of its *-chen* suffix. When you add the *-chen* suffix to a German noun, that noun automatically becomes grammatically neuter, regardless of the noun's meaning. The word **Mädchen** is a good example of how natural gender and grammatical gender are two separate concepts.

Since **Mädchen** is a neuter noun, if you want to put *the* in front of it, you must use the neuter form, which is **das**. And when you memorize it, say it along with its article, like this: **das Mädchen**.

EXERCISES

1. **Mädchen**
2. **Das Mädchen**
3. **Frau**
4. **Die Frau**
5. **Mann**
6. **Der Mann**

Answers on page 189.

LESSON 13

SINGULAR AND PLURAL

Singular means there is one of something.

Plural means there is more than one of something.

Just for practice, try to figure out if the underlined word in each sentence is singular or plural.

EXERCISES

1. I have three <u>cats</u>.
2. Hand me that <u>book</u>, please.
3. I saw a <u>deer</u> in the woods.
4. I want to catch a <u>fish</u>.
5. There are many <u>cars</u> on the road today.
6. I need a new <u>pair</u> of pants.
7. The <u>deer</u> are eating all of my plants!
8. We don't have any more <u>cookies</u>.
9. The <u>fish</u> are in the fishbowl.
10. We painted the wrong <u>house</u>.

Answers on page 189.

LESSON 14

WAYS TO MAKE NOUNS PLURAL

In English, to make a noun plural we generally just add an *s* to the end of the word. But in German, there are several kinds of spelling changes that can be applied to nouns to make them plural. In this lesson, we will introduce you to some of these spelling changes.

Since English is a Germanic language, we have some old nouns in English that form their plurals like German words. Using these archaic words as examples, let's try to observe some of the various ways of making German nouns plural.

VOWEL CHANGE ONLY

In German, some nouns are made plural just by changing the sound of the vowel within the word. We have a few words in English that behave this way, such as these:

- foot ⟶ feet
- goose ⟶ geese
- woman ⟶ women
- man ⟶ men
- mouse ⟶ mice
- tooth ⟶ teeth

ADDING -EN

In German, some nouns become plural by adding *-en* to the end of the noun. We could only think of one English word that does this—the word *ox*.

ox ⟶ oxen

BOTH A VOWEL CHANGE AND ADDING -EN

In German, some nouns become plural by getting both a vowel change and a new ending, which is *-en*. We have a small number of words in English that do the same thing, such as the word *child*.

13

child ⟶ children

Also, there's the word *brethren*, which is an archaic plural for the word *brother*.

brother ⟶ brethren

NO CHANGE

In German, some nouns are spelled the same and sound the same in both their singular and plural forms. And some English nouns behave like that too. Since there is no difference in sound or spelling between the singular form and the plural form, you must use the context to determine if these words are singular or plural.

- fish ⟶ fish
- moose ⟶ moose
- deer ⟶ deer
- sheep ⟶ sheep

ADDING -S

In German, there are some words that form their plural by adding -*s*. This mostly happens with words borrowed from other languages. So when you see a German noun that has been borrowed from, say for instance, English, it will probably make its plural form just by adding an *s*. Of course, we do this in English all the time, like this:

- dog ⟶ dogs
- cat ⟶ cats

Again, this lesson has been just a warm-up to get you ready to study real German plurals in the next lesson. The English words we gave above represent several of the different ways that German nouns can be made plural—but there are a couple more that we will point out to you as we go along.

LESSON 15

PLURAL NOUNS IN GERMAN

In the last lesson, using carefully selected English words, we looked at a few of the ways in which German nouns are made plural. Now that we have observed some of these methods, let's see how these methods work by studying some actual German nouns.

VOWEL CHANGE

The German word for *brother* is **Bruder** (it sounds something like *BROO-dah*, with a gargling *r* sound in the back of the mouth). Like the English words *goose* and *tooth*, this particular noun is an example of a noun that forms its plural just by changing the vowel sound within the word.

Bruder ⟶ Brüder

Notice that in the plural form there is an **Umlaut** over the letter *u* which indicates a change in the sound of the vowel. It makes the letter *u* sound something like the -*ew* in the English word *few*. When you make this vowel sound, form your lips into a rounded shape. Therefore the plural **Brüder** sounds something like *BREW-dah*.

ADDING -EN

You already know the word **Frau** which means *woman*. Like the English word *ox*, the German word **Frau** forms its plural by adding -*en*.

Frau ⟶ Frauen

NO CHANGE

You already know **Mädchen**, the German word for *girl*. Like the English word *deer*, the German word **Mädchen** looks and sounds the same in both the singular and plural forms. If you see it in a sentence, you must use the context to determine whether it is singular or plural.

Mädchen ⟶ Mädchen

15

BOTH A VOWEL CHANGE AND ADDING -ER

The word **Mann** forms its plural through both a vowel sound change and by adding -*er* to the end.

Mann ⟶ Männer

Notice that in the plural form there is an **Umlaut** over the letter *a* which indicates a change in the sound of the vowel. This **Umlaut** makes the letter *a* sound something like the *e* in *bed*. Therefore plural **Männer** sounds something like *MEN-nah*.

ADDING -S

The German language contains many words borrowed from other languages such as English. For example, the English word *baby* has been borrowed into German. Observe how it forms its plural.

Baby ⟶ Babys

In English, we would make the word *baby* plural by making it *babies*, with -*ies* at the end, but in German, as a loan word, the word **Baby** is made plural simply by adding an *s*. Be sure to watch out for this kind of spelling whenever you see German words that have been borrowed from other languages.

We have now covered most of the ways that German nouns can become plural. There are a couple of other ways, but we don't need to talk about those right now— we will address them in the future when needed.

LESSON 16

PLURAL ARTICLES

We have already studied singular articles, and you know that there is a different word for masculine *the*, feminine *the*, and neuter *the*. But in the plural, there isn't a separate article for each gender. Instead, the same word serves as the plural article for all three genders. This plural article is the word **die** (pronounced *dee*).

Now you might be saying to yourself, "Hey, wait a minute—I thought the word **die** was the feminine singular form of the word *the*, and now you're saying it's also the plural form of *the*??" Yes, that's right—**die** is both the feminine form of the word *the* and the plural form of *the* for all genders. We know that this can be confusing to those of you who are new to German, but you'll get used to it with practice.

Let's start working with the plural article **die**. Observe the word **die** being used to introduce each of the nouns you know so far, but in their plural form. We have one of each gender: masculine, feminine, and neuter.

- **die Männer** *(the men)*
- **die Frauen** *(the woman)*
- **die Mädchen** *(the girls)*

This handy chart shows all the forms of *the* that we have learned so far:

MASCULINE	FEMININE	NEUTER	PLURAL
der	**die**	**das**	**die**

same

EXERCISES

1. **Der Mann** The man
2. **Die Männer** The men
3. **Die Frau** The woman

4. **Die Frauen** The women
5. **Das Mädchen** the girl
6. **Die Mädchen** the girls

Answers on page 189.

LESSON 17

NEW WORD **Junge**

MEANING *boy*

PRONUNCIATION TIP: **Junge** has two syllables. The letter *j* at the beginning makes a *yuh* sound, so it sounds something like *YOON-guh*.

Junge is a masculine noun, so it needs to have the masculine article **der**.

To form the plural of **Junge**, simply add the letter *n*:

Junge ⟶ Jungen

So if you want to say *the boy* it would be **der Junge** and if you want to say *the boys* it would be **die Jungen**.

In everyday speech you might hear a less formal plural form of **Junge** which is **Jungs**. In written German though, you'll see **Jungen**.

EXERCISES

1. **Der Junge** The boy
2. **Die Jungen** The boys
3. **Der Mann** The man
4. **Die Männer** The men
5. **Die Frau** The woman
6. **Die Frauen** The women
7. **Das Mädchen** The girl
8. **Die Mädchen** The girls

Answers on page 189.

LESSON 18

NEW WORD   **und**

MEANING   *and*

PRONUNCIATION TIP: Remember that when it comes at the end of a word, the letter *d* sounds like a *t*. So **und** sounds something like *oont*.

EXERCISES

1. **Der Junge und das Mädchen** *The boy and the girl*
2. **Die Mädchen und die Jungen** *The girls and the boys*
3. **Die Frau und der Mann** *The woman and the man*
4. **Die Frauen und die Männer** *The women and the men*
5. **Das Mädchen und die Frau** *The girl and the woman*
6. **Der Junge und der Mann** *The boy & the man*
7. **Die Frauen und die Mädchen** *The women and the girls*
8. **Das Mädchen** *The girl*
9. **Die Jungen** *The boys*
10. **Der Junge** *The boy*

Answers on page 189.

LESSON 19

MORE ABOUT ARTICLES

At the beginning of this book we learned a little something about articles. We learned that articles are words like *the*, *a*, and *an*, and we learned to use them to introduce nouns. Now, as we move ahead to the next steps of German grammar, we need to tell you some additional information about articles. In this lesson we want to discuss the difference between definite articles and indefinite articles.

In English, the word *the* is called the *definite article*. Why? Because when you use it, you are referring to a definite thing. Here's an example:

Please go into the garage and get the broom.

When you make a statement like this, it is clear that you are referring not to just any broom—instead, you have a specific broom in mind, and you want someone to go and get it! You are referring to a definite thing, therefore *the* is a definite article. In German, **der**, **die**, and **das** are definite articles.

Even when plural, the definite article still works the same way.

Please go into the garage and get the brooms.

Here, even though you are referring to more than one broom, you still have specific brooms in mind. In German, the plural definite article is **die**.

In English, the words *a* and *an* are called *indefinite articles*. Why? Because they don't refer to any specific item. Instead, they just refer to any item that fits the description. Here's an example:

Please go into the garage and get a broom.

When you make a statement like this, you are not referring to any specific broom. In fact, there may be several brooms in the garage, and you are just asking someone to go and pick one—any broom will do. The thing you are asking for is indefinite, therefore *a* and *an* are indefinite articles.

The word *the* can be used to talk about something singular or something plural. In other words, the word *the* functions as both a singular article and a plural article.

But *a* and *an* cannot function as plural articles the way the word *the* can. You cannot say *a brooms* or *an apples*. So, if you are an English speaker, what do you do when you need a plural indefinite article? When we need an indefinite article to be plural, we express the plural-ness of it by using the word *some*. Here's an example:

Please go into the garage and get <u>some</u> brooms.

When you make a statement like this, you are not using the word *some* as the opposite of the word *all*, as if to say, "Don't get all of the brooms—make sure you leave a few behind." That's not the point. Instead, the word *some* here is functioning as a plural indefinite article—in other words, a plural form of *a* or *an*. What you mean is that it doesn't matter which brooms the person gets—he or she just needs to get several or a few brooms.

So far, you know about German definite articles, but we haven't covered indefinite articles yet. In the next lesson you will start to work with indefinite articles in German.

LESSON 20

NEW WORD   **ein**

MEANING   *a, an*

PRONUNCIATION TIP: **Ein** sounds like the word *mine* but without the *m*.

We already know how to say *the* in German, and now it's time to learn how to say *a* and *an*.

In German, as you might expect, there are different words for the different genders of *a* and *an*. In this lesson we are only studying the masculine form, which is

ein. So that means that in this lesson, we will just be practicing using **ein** and masculine nouns.

Masculine	Feminine	Neuter
ein		

Here are some examples of how to use **ein**:

- **ein Mann** *(a man)*
- **ein Junge** *(a boy)*

EXERCISES

1. **Ein Mann** a man
2. **Ein Mann und ein Junge** a man and a boy
3. **Die Frauen und ein Mann** The women and a man
4. **Ein Junge und ein Mann** A boy and a man
5. **Die Mädchen und der Junge** The girls and the boy
6. **Die Frau und ein Mann** The woman and a man
7. **Die Männer und die Jungen** The men and the boys
8. **Das Mädchen** The girl
9. **Die Frau und ein Junge** The woman and a boy
10. **Die Mädchen und ein Junge** The girls and a boy

Answers on page 189.

LESSON 21

NEW WORD   **eine**

MEANING   *a, an*

PRONUNCIATION TIP: **Eine** has two syllables, so it sounds something like *EYE-nuh.*

In the last lesson, you learned that **ein** is the masculine form of *a* and *an.* In this lesson, we will learn the feminine form which is **eine.** We use it to say *a* or *an* before feminine nouns. Examine the following chart:

MASCULINE	FEMININE	NEUTER
ein	**eine**	

Here's an example of how to use **eine:**

    eine Frau *(a woman)*

EXERCISES

1. **Eine Frau**
2. **Eine Frau und ein Mann**
3. **Die Frauen und ein Mann**
4. **Die Männer**
5. **Das Mädchen und ein Junge**
6. **Die Mädchen und eine Frau**
7. **Die Jungen und die Frau**
8. **Die Männer und ein Junge**
9. **Ein Mann und eine Frau**
10. **Das Mädchen und eine Frau**

Answers on page 189.

LESSON 22

MORE ABOUT EIN

Now that you know the masculine and feminine forms of *a* and *an*, it's time to learn the neuter form.

The neuter form of *a* and *an* is **ein**. So this means that the neuter form is the same as the masculine form (but don't let that confuse you). Examine the following chart:

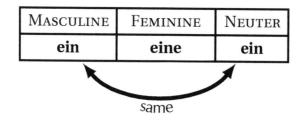

Masculine	Feminine	Neuter
ein	**eine**	**ein**

same

So if you have a neuter noun, you need to use the neuter form of **ein**, like this:

> **ein Mädchen** *(a girl)*

EXERCISES

1. **Das Mädchen**
2. **Ein Mädchen**
3. **Eine Frau und ein Mädchen**
4. **Die Mädchen und die Jungen**
5. **Die Frauen und der Mann**
6. **Eine Frau und ein Mann**
7. **Ein Mädchen und ein Junge**
8. **Der Mann und die Frau**
9. **Die Frauen und die Männer**
10. **Der Junge und ein Mann**

Answers on page 189.

LESSON 23

PLURAL FORMS OF EIN?

As we explained a few lesson ago, there are definite articles and indefinite articles. In German, the definite articles are **der**, **die**, **das**, and **die**. The indefinite articles are **ein**, **eine**, and **ein**.

In this lesson, let's talk about plural indefinite articles. We have already discussed singular indefinite articles—in English, the words *a* and *an*. But *a* and *an* don't have plural forms. So in English we tend to express an plural indefinite article by using the word *some*. Observe these examples of singular indefinite articles followed by their plural counterparts:

- a pencil ⟶ some pencils

- a car ⟶ some cars

But how would we express this kind of thing in German? In other words, how would we say something like *some men* or *some girls* in German? Observe this chart:

MASCULINE	FEMININE	NEUTER	PLURAL
ein	**eine**	**ein**	*doesn't exist*

WHAAAT?

Unfortunately, there are no plural forms of **ein** in German. So if you want to say something like *I have some books* in German you could say (as a word-for-word translation) *I have books*. When you say *I have books* in German, that is saying roughly the same thing as what we would be expressing when we say *I have some books* in English.

Of course you don't know how to say all this in German yet, but for now we at least wanted you to understand the concept of plural indefinite articles just for your knowledge. We will address this topic again in the future when needed.

LESSON 24

NEW WORD   **Bruder**

MEANING   *brother*

PRONUNCIATION TIP: **Bruder** has a gurgling *r* at the beginning and an open *r* at the end, so it sounds something like *BROO-dah*.

Bruder is masculine, so it needs to have a masculine article such as **der** or **ein**. It forms its plural with only a vowel change, like this:

Bruder ⟶ Brüder

Notice the **Umlaut** over the *u* in the plural form. That changes the vowel sound from a regular *u* to the kind of sound in the word *few*—the kind you make with your lips rounded. This is an example of a time when it is important to listen carefully to the pronunciation recordings and copy what you hear.

EXERCISES

1. **Der Bruder**
2. **Die Brüder**
3. **Ein Bruder**
4. **Die Frau und der Mann**
5. **Das Mädchen und ein Junge**
6. **Eine Frau und ein Mann**
7. **Die Jungen und die Frauen**
8. **Der Junge und die Frau**
9. **Die Männer und die Mädchen**
10. **Der Mann und die Frauen**

Answers on page 189.

LESSON 25

NEW WORD   **Schwester**

MEANING   *sister*

PRONUNCIATION TIP: The *w* here sounds like a *v*, and the *r* at the end has an open *r* sound. So this word will sound something like *SHVESS-tah*.

Schwester is a feminine noun, so it needs to have a feminine article such as **die** or **eine**.

To make **Schwester** plural, just add an *n*:

Schwester ⟶ **Schwestern**

EXERCISES

1. **Eine Schwester und ein Bruder**
2. **Der Bruder und die Schwester**
3. **Die Schwestern und die Brüder**
4. **Das Mädchen und der Junge**
5. **Ein Mädchen und ein Junge**
6. **Die Jungen und die Mädchen**
7. **Die Frau und der Mann**
8. **Die Männer und die Frauen**
9. **Die Frauen und die Mädchen**
10. **Die Jungen und das Mädchen**

Answers on page 189.

LESSON 26

NEW WORD   **Freund**

MEANING   *friend* (male)

PRONUNCIATION TIP: The *r* sound is the gargling kind, and the *d* at the end sounds like a *t*. So **Freund** sounds something like *froint*.

Freund is a masculine noun, so it needs to have a masculine article such as **der** or **ein**.

In German there are separate words for *male friend* and *female friend*. **Freund** is the word for a *male friend*.

Do you remember way back in lesson 15 when we discussed the different ways that nouns can be made plural? We said that there were other ways of making nouns plural that we would discuss in the future. Well, the future is now! In order to make **Freund** plural, you have to add the letter *e* to the end, like this:

     Freund ⟶ Freunde

Freunde sounds something like *FROYN-deh*.

EXERCISES

1. **Die Brüder und die Freunde**
2. **Die Schwestern und der Freund**
3. **Ein Freund**
4. **Der Freund**
5. **Die Freunde**
6. **Ein Bruder und eine Schwester**
7. **Die Frau und die Männer**
8. **Das Mädchen und die Jungen**
9. **Ein Mädchen und ein Junge**
10. **Die Mädchen und eine Frau**

Answers on page 190.

28

LESSON 27

NEW WORD   **Freundin**

MEANING   *friend* (female)

To form the plural of **Freundin** (*female friend*) add *-en*. But in addition to that, you also have to add in an extra *n*, like this:

Freundin ⟶ Freundinnen

Here's a convenient chart so you can review all four forms of the German word for *friend*.

	SINGULAR	PLURAL
MALE	**Freund**	**Freunde**
FEMALE	**Freundin**	**Freundinnen**

One last thing—if you have a group of friends that is comprised of both males and females, you would use the masculine plural, calling them **Freunde**.

EXERCISES

1. **Die Freundin**
2. **Die Freundinnen**
3. **Der Freund**
4. **Die Freunde**
5. **Die Schwestern und ein Bruder**
6. **Die Brüder und die Schwester**
7. **Das Mädchen und eine Frau**
8. **Die Mädchen und die Jungen**
9. **Der Junge und ein Mädchen**
10. **Der Mann und die Frauen**

Answers on page 190.

LESSON 28

NEW WORD   **mein**

MEANING   *my*

PRONUNCIATION TIP: **Mein** sounds like *mine*, not *main*.

In English, the word *my* is always the same. But in German, there is a masculine, feminine, neuter, and even plural form of the word for *my*. Observe these forms in the chart below:

MASCULINE	FEMININE	NEUTER	PLURAL
mein	**meine**	**mein**	**meine**

Notice how similar these forms are to the various forms of **ein**. Compare them below.

MASCULINE	FEMININE	NEUTER	PLURAL
ein	**eine**	**ein**	*doesn't exist*

WUT?

So **mein** is just like **ein**, but with an *m* stuck to the front. But notice the important difference—although **ein** does not have a plural form, **mein** does.

EXERCISES

1. **Mein Bruder und meine Schwester**
2. **Meine Schwester und meine Brüder**
3. **Meine Freundin**
4. **Meine Freundinnen**
5. **Meine Schwester und ein Freund**
6. **Das Mädchen und der Junge**
7. **Die Freunde**
8. **Die Frauen und ein Freund**
9. **Meine Brüder und mein Freund**
10. **Meine Schwester und eine Frau**

Answers on page 190.

LESSON 29

MORE ABOUT MANN AND FRAU

Mann means *man*, but it can also mean *husband*. So, if you see **Mann** in a sentence, how do you know whether it means *man* or *husband*? The answer is to look at the context—that is, the way the word is being used in the sentence. Let's say, for example, you see this:

The **Mann** went to the store.

It is perfectly normal to say *the man went to the store*, but a lot less likely that someone would say *the husband went to the store*. Therefore, if you saw a sentence like this one, you could judge from the context that the word **Mann** here probably means *man*, not *husband*. Here's another example:

My **Mann** went to the store.

Here, the use of the word *my* changes the context, or the way the word is being used. It is perfectly normal to say *my husband went to the store*, but less likely that someone would say *my man went to the store*. Therefore, if you saw a sentence like this one, you could judge from the context that the word **Mann** here probably means *husband*, not *man*.

To summarize, if you see the **Mann** being introduced by **der** or **ein**, it probably means *man*, and if you see it being introduced by a possessive word like *my, your, his, her,* etc., it probably means *husband*.

The word **Frau** is the same way. It can mean either *woman* or *wife*, depending on the way it is used. If you see **Frau** introduced by an article like *the* or *a*, it probably means *woman*. If you see it with a possessive word, it probably means *wife*.

EXERCISES

1. **Der Mann**
2. **Mein Mann**
3. **Eine Frau**
4. **Meine Frau**
5. **Meine Freundin und meine Frau**
6. **Meine Brüder und mein Mann**
7. **Die Brüder und meine Schwestern**
8. **Meine Freundinnen und ein Junge**
9. **Meine Schwestern und das Mädchen**
10. **Meine Frau und die Jungen**

Answers on page 190.

LESSON 30

MORE ABOUT FREUND AND FREUNDIN

In the last lesson we saw that using words like *my* and *your* with **Mann** and **Frau** changed their meaning. If you say **Mann**, it just means *man*, but if you say **mein Mann**, it means *my husband*. Likewise, if you just say **Frau**, it means *woman*, but if you say **meine Frau** it means *my wife*.

The same thing happens with the German words for *friend*, which are **Freund** (male friend) and **Freundin** (female friend). These words can simply mean *friend*, but if you put possessive words like **mein** with them, it can have the meaning of *boyfriend* or *girlfriend*. So if you are speaking German and you say **mein Freund**, it is ambiguous—the person you are talking to could interpret it to mean *my friend* or *my boyfriend*. You may have to explain further in order for the listener to know exactly what you mean.

Likewise, if you are speaking German and you say **meine Freundin**, this is also ambiguous. The person you are speaking to could interpret it to mean *my friend* or *my girlfriend*. You may have to explain further in order for the listener to know exactly what you mean.

Therefore, context is key. When you hear the context in which a word is being used, it helps you understand what the speaker is trying to express. This book is for beginners, and for that reason the exercises are rather short—and since they are short, they do not provide much context. For this reason, in the answer key, whenever we use the words **Freund** or **Freundin** with words like *my, your, his,* or *her*, we will add in extra words to show that there might be more than one meaning, or to clear up any ambiguity. For example, if you see this exercise...

meine Freundin

...if the context calls for it, we may translate it in the answer key like this:

(female) *friend/girlfriend*

In this way, we will try to remove any guesswork or confusion that might arise from these ambiguous words so you can understand their full range of meanings right from the start.

LESSON 31

NEW WORD   **Sohn**

MEANING   *son*

PRONUNCIATION TIP: This word sounds something like *zone*.

To form the plural of **Sohn**, we add *e* to the end, but there is also a vowel change. Here it is:

Sohn ⟶ **Söhne**

Notice that in the plural form, the **Umlaut** changes the sound of the vowel. This sound is like the *e* in *bed*, but with your lips rounded, so **Söhne** sounds something like *ZUH-nuh* or maybe *ZUR-nuh*. Listen carefully to the pronunciation recordings to try to copy this sound.

EXERCISES

1. **Mein Sohn**
2. **Meine Söhne**
3. **Mein Freund und meine Frau**
4. **Meine Schwester und meine Söhne**
5. **Mein Sohn und meine Freundin**
6. **Mein Mann und meine Schwester**
7. **Der Freund und der Junge**
8. **Mein Bruder, meine Söhne und meine Freundin**
9. **Mein Sohn und ein Mädchen**
10. **Meine Freundinnen und eine Frau**

Answers on page 190.

LESSON 32

NEW WORD   **Tochter**

MEANING   *daughter*

PRONUNCIATION TIP: The *ch* in **Tochter** is a scraping sound you make in the back of your mouth, not a *k* sound.

The plural of **Tochter** is formed with only a vowel change, indicated by an **Umlaut**.

     Tochter ⟶ Töchter

In the plural form, the *o* with the **Umlaut** over it sounds like saying the *e* in *bed*, but with your lips rounded. Also, the *ch* sound is different in the plural form. Here, it sounds more like the whooshing sound of air passing over the tongue like at the beginning of the word *huge*. So **Töchter** sounds something like *TURSH-tah*.

EXERCISES

1. **Meine Tochter**
2. **Meine Töchter**
3. **Ein Sohn und eine Tochter**
4. **Meine Schwestern und meine Töchter**
5. **Mein Mann und mein Bruder**
6. **Meine Freundin und meine Frau**
7. **Die Jungen und das Mädchen**
8. **Der Junge und die Männer**
9. **Die Frau und mein Freund**
10. **Ein Mädchen und ein Junge**

Answers on page 190.

LESSON 33

EIN-WORDS

Now that you've been working with the word **ein** for a few lessons, it's time for you to learn more about the word **ein** and its pattern of endings.

In German, there is an entire group of words that share the same pattern of endings as **ein**. We call these words **ein**-words. You have already seen one **ein**-word, and that is the word **mein**.

As we mentioned before, **mein** is very similar to **ein**. It's so similar in fact, that it's just as if you took the letter *m* and stuck it to the front of **ein**. The only difference (and this is a big one) is that **ein**-words such as **mein** do have a plural form while **ein** itself does not.

Throughout the book, as you continue to learn more **ein** words, you'll see that same pattern of endings over and over again. These words will be possessive adjectives—that is, the German words for *your, his, her, its, our,* and *their.*

LESSON 34

NEW WORD   **dein**

MEANING   *your*

PRONUNCIATION TIP: **Dein** sounds like *dine*.

In the last lesson, you learned that in German there is an entire group of words called *ein-words*. Our new word for this lesson is another **ein**-word. As you can see in the following chart, it follows the same pattern as **ein** and **mein**.

Masculine	Feminine	Neuter	Plural
dein	**deine**	**dein**	**deine**

EXERCISES

1. **Dein Freund**
2. **Deine Schwester**
3. **Deine Freundinnen und meine Töchter**
4. **Deine Brüder und meine Schwestern**
5. **Deine Freundin und meine Schwester**
6. **Ein Freund und eine Freundin**
7. **Deine Tochter und mein Sohn**
8. **Der Junge und meine Freundin**
9. **Das Mädchen und die Jungen**
10. **Die Männer und deine Söhne**

Answers on page 190.

LESSON 35

NEW WORD **Eltern**

MEANING *parents*

Our new word for this lesson is mostly just used in the plural, so you will see sentences like this:

meine Eltern *(my parents)*

EXERCISES

1. **Die Eltern**
2. **Meine Eltern und deine Eltern**
3. **Deine Söhne und Töchter**
4. **Die Frauen und meine Frau**
5. **Meine Freundinnen**
6. **Meine Freunde**
7. **Deine Schwester und deine Freunde**
8. **Meine Töchter und dein Bruder**
9. **Das Mädchen und die Jungen**
10. **Mein Mann und meine Schwestern**

Answers on page 191.

LESSON 36

NEW WORD **Kind**

MEANING *child*

PRONUNCIATION TIP: The word **Kind** rhymes with *bent* and *mint*.

The word **Kind** is grammatically neuter, even though according to natural gender a child would be either male or female.

To form the plural we just add *-er*, like this:

Kind ⟶ **Kinder**

In the plural form, the *d* is pronounced like the *d* in *dog*, so it sounds something like *KIN-dah*.

You can use the word **Kind** just as we use the word *child* in English.

- To refer to any child, like this: **das Kind** (*the child*)
- To refer to *offspring*, as in sons and daughters: **meine Kinder** (*my children*)

EXERCISES

1. **Ein Kind**
2. **Meine Kinder**
3. **Meine Tochter und deine Freundinnen**
4. **Meine Eltern und mein Mann**
5. **Deine Schwestern und die Kinder**
6. **Mein Sohn und die Jungen**
7. **Das Kind und die Frau**
8. **Deine Frau und deine Schwestern**
9. **Ein Mann und eine Frau**
10. **Meine Töchter und meine Brüder**

Answers on page 191.

LESSON 37

NEW WORD **guten Tag / auf Wiedersehen**

MEANING *good day / see you later*

PRONUNCIATION TIP: The *g* in **Tag** sounds like a *k*. **Wiedersehen** sounds something like *VEE-duh-zay-in*.

Guten means *good*, and **Tag** means *day*, so **guten Tag** literally means *good day*. It's the standard German way of saying *Hello*.

Auf means *until*. The verb **sehen** means *to see* or *seeing*. The word **wieder** means *again*. So **auf Wiedersehen** literally means something like *until seeing again*. But we commonly translate it into English as *goodbye*. In this book we will translate it as *see you later* because that is closer to its true meaning than simply *goodbye*. Other common greetings are **guten Abend**, which means *good evening*, and **guten Morgen**, which means *good morning*.

Gute Nacht means *good night*, as in the kind of thing you would say before going to bed at night. Notice that while the other expressions in this lesson have the adjective **guten**, this particular expression has **gute** instead. Since **Tag** and **Abend** are masculine nouns, they have the masculine form of the adjective: **guten**. But since **Nacht** is a feminine noun, it must have the feminine form of the adjective which is **gute**. We won't cover adjectives in this book, but you should at least be aware that in German, an adjective will change form depending on its gender and number.

EXERCISES

1. **Guten Tag, mein Freund.**
2. **Auf Wiedersehen, mein Sohn.**
3. **Guten Abend, meine Freunde.**
4. **Meine Tochter und deine Schwester.**
5. **Der Mann und meine Brüder.**
6. **Meine Eltern und deine Eltern.**
7. **Deine Söhne und die Kinder.**
8. **Die Frau und das Kind.**
9. **Ein Junge und ein Mädchen.**
10. **Deine Frau und deine Freundinnen**

Answers on page 191.

LESSON 38

NEW WORD   **Vater / Mutter**

MEANING   *father / mother*

PRONUNCIATION TIP: In German, a *v* makes an *f* sound, so **Vater** sounds something like *FAH-tah.* **Mutter** sounds something like *MUH-tah.*

Our new words for this lesson form their plurals with only a vowel change, as indicated by an **Umlaut:**

- **Vater ⟶ Väter**

- **Mutter ⟶ Mütter**

In the plural form of **Mutter**, listen for a slight change in the vowel sound, which comes from rounding the lips. Therefore it should sound something like *MUR-tah.* In the plural form of **Vater**, the vowel change is more obvious, and **Väter** sounds something like *FAY-tah.*

So the German words for *father, mother, son,* and *daughter* all form their plurals the same way, with an **Umlaut.**

EXERCISES

1. **Mein Vater und meine Mutter.**
2. **Deine Mutter und dein Vater.**
3. **Die Väter und die Mütter.**
4. **Guten Tag, Kinder.**
5. **Auf Wiedersehen, Mutter.**
6. **Die Männer und die Jungen.**
7. **Meine Schwestern, meine Tochter, und meine Eltern.**
8. **Deine Mutter und eine Freundin.**
9. **Der Mann und deine Brüder.**
10. **Das Kind und meine Söhne.**

Answers on page 191.

40

LESSON 39

SUBJECTS AND VERBS

In any sentence, the two most important elements are the subject and the verb. Let's take a moment now to think about how subjects and verbs work.

A noun is a person, place, or thing. The subject of a sentence is the noun that is doing the action in the sentence. In each of the following examples, the underlined word is the subject of the sentence.

- <u>Matthew</u> kicked the ball.
- <u>Canada</u> is a large country.
- <u>Flowers</u> need sunshine.

Now let's talk about verbs. Verbs are words that tell us what the subject of the sentence is doing. Verbs can be action words such as *dance, shout, walk, talk* or *write.* Or, they can be verbs of being or existing such as *is, are, was, were,* and *will be.* Verbs of being are also called *linking verbs.* Let's look at those same sentences again, this time underlining the verb in each sentence.

- Matthew <u>kicked</u> the ball.
- Canada <u>is</u> a large country.
- Flowers <u>need</u> sunshine.

For practice, see if you can identify the subject and verb of each of the following sentences.

EXERCISES

1. Kate walks to school every day.
2. My car is red.
3. My sister likes ice cream.
4. The horse is brown.
5. Harry told me a joke.
6. On Thursdays, Bob plays softball.
7. Mark plays the trumpet.
8. My brother never cleans his room.
9. Julia loves bedtime stories.
10. The students finished their homework.

Answers on page 191.

LESSON 40

PRONOUNS

A pronoun is a word that can take the place of a noun. Pronouns are words like *he, she, it, I, we, you* and *they*. We often use pronouns when we have already used a certain noun once and do not want to say that same noun again.

Here is an example of how we use pronouns in everyday speech.

Susanne is wearing a blue dress. <u>She</u> bought it last week.

Let's look at that last example again, this time without the word *she*.

Susanne is wearing a blue dress. <u>Susanne</u> bought it last week.

That example did not sound as good because the noun *Susanne* was repeated. So you can see how useful pronouns can be in everyday conversation.

In each of the following exercises, try to identify the pronoun. And, if the pronoun is taking the place of another word, identify that word also.

EXERCISES

1. Alfred's room is a mess because he never cleans up.
2. Jeff does not like going to the locker room because it is too smelly.
3. She already took out the trash.
4. The kids want to come inside because they are cold.
5. The teacher told Johnny to stop, but he didn't listen.
6. We are going to the beach.
7. They are not going to the party.
8. You are sitting in the wrong chair.
9. The rabbit was scared, so it ran away.
10. Don't disturb the children; they are asleep.

Answers on page 191.

LESSON 41

NEW WORD   **ich bin**

MEANING   *I am*

PRONUNCIATION TIP: In the word **ich**, the *ch* sounds like the sound of air whooshing over your tongue.

This is a special lesson because here we are learning our first German pronoun and our first German verb. The word **ich** is a pronoun that means *I*, and **bin** is the verb which means *am*. **Ich** is not capitalized unless it is the first word in a sentence.

Now that you know your first verb, we can make complete German sentences (try not to get too excited).

EXERCISES

1. **Ich bin ein Kind.**
2. **Ich bin dein Bruder.**
3. **Ich bin deine Mutter.**
4. **Ich bin ein Mann.**
5. **Ich bin dein Mann.**
6. **Die Kinder und die Eltern.**
7. **Guten Tag, Mütter und Väter.**
8. **Meine Kinder, meine Frau und meine Eltern.**
9. **Mein Vater und mein Sohn.**
10. **Ein Mädchen und ein Junge.**

Answers on page 191.

LESSON 42

NEW WORD   **nicht**

MEANING   *not*

PRONUNCIATION TIP: The *ch* in **nicht** sounds like the beginning of the word *huge*.

When you negate a verb, you indicate that the action of the verb is not happening. In English, we use the word *not* to negate a verb.

- I am your brother.
- I am <u>not</u> your brother.

In German, we use the word **nicht** to negate a verb, just as we would use the word *not* in English. In the simple sentences we are making right now, the word **nicht** will go right after the verb. Here's an example:

Ich bin <u>nicht</u> deine Schwester. *(I am <u>not</u> your sister.)*

In a German sentence, the order of the words can be different and more complicated than it would be in a similar English sentence. Therefore, in a German sentence, the word **nicht** can be put in different places. So, for the moment, practice with these simple sentences, and as we go along we will tell you more about how you can use **nicht** in a sentence.

EXERCISES

1. **Ich bin.**
2. **Ich bin nicht dein Kind!**
3. **Ich bin nicht dein Bruder.**
4. **Auf Wiedersehen, meine Freundin.**
5. **Ich bin nicht deine Mutter.**
6. **Mein Vater und meine Frau.**
7. **Guten Tag, meine Kinder.**
8. **Meine Eltern und meine Tochter.**
9. **Mein Kind und die Mädchen.**
10. **Guten Abend, Mutter und Vater.**

Answers on page 191.

LESSON 43

NEW WORD   **du bist**

MEANING   *you are*

Du is a pronoun, which means *you* (singular). **Bist** is a verb, which means *are.*

Du bist mein Freund. *(You are my friend.)*

EXERCISES

1. **Du bist meine Freundin.**
2. **Du bist nicht mein Bruder.**
3. **Ich bin deine Schwester.**
4. **Ich bin deine Mutter.**
5. **Guten Tag, meine Söhne.**
6. **Ich bin deine Tochter. Ich bin nicht dein Sohn.**
7. **Mein Vater und dein Bruder.**
8. **Meine Eltern und meine Freunde.**
9. **Eine Frau und meine Schwestern.**
10. **Meine Töchter, mein Sohn, die Männer und die Kinder.**

Answers on page 192.

LESSON 44

NEW WORD   **ist**

MEANING   *is*

Ist simply means *is.* It is just like the English word *is.*

     Das Mädchen ist meine Schwester. *(The girl is my sister.)*

EXERCISES

1. **Der Mann ist mein Vater.**
2. **Die Frau ist meine Mutter.**
3. **Meine Schwester ist nicht deine Freundin.**
4. **Mein Sohn ist dein Freund.**
5. **Das Kind ist nicht mein Bruder.**
6. **Du bist meine Freundin.**
7. **Guten Tag, Väter und Mütter.**
8. **Deine Frau ist meine Schwester.**
9. **Meine Freundinnen und deine Eltern.**
10. **Ich bin ein Junge.**

Answers on page 192.

LESSON 45

NEW WORD   **er**

MEANING   *he*

PRONUNCIATION TIP: **Er** has an open *r* sound, so pronounce it something like *e-ah*.

Er is a masculine pronoun that means *he*.

EXERCISES

1. **Er ist mein Vater.**
2. **Er ist nicht mein Bruder.**
3. **Er ist mein Kind.**
4. **Anette ist meine Mutter und Fritz ist mein Vater.**
5. **Du bist nicht mein Bruder.**
6. **Ich bin dein Vater.**
7. **Meine Eltern, deine Frau und die Kinder.**
8. **Dein Bruder und eine Freundin.**
9. **Meine Schwester und eine Frau.**
10. **Auf Wiedersehen, mein Freund.**

Answers on page 192.

LESSON 46

NEW WORD **sie**

MEANING *she*

PRONUNCIATION TIP: **Sie** sounds like *zee*.

Sie is a feminine pronoun that means *she*.

EXERCISES

1. **Sie ist meine Schwester.**
2. **Sie ist meine Mutter.**
3. **Sie ist nicht meine Tochter.**
4. **Sie ist meine Freundin.**
5. **Auf Wiedersehen, Mutter.**
6. **Er ist mein Freund.**
7. **Er ist nicht mein Kind.**
8. **Ich bin dein Bruder.**
9. **Du bist mein Vater.**
10. **Das Mädchen ist nicht meine Tochter.**

Answers on page 192.

LESSON 47

NEW WORD   **es**

MEANING   *it*

The German word **es** is just like our English word *it.* It can be used in sentences in many of the same ways that you would use the word *it* in an English sentence. Consider these English sentences which use the word *it:*

- There is my suitcase! Grab it!
- It is morning.
- It is raining.
- It is too early!
- Where is it?
- Who is it?

So you see, in English we use the word *it* in various ways. We can use it to refer to an inanimate object, such as a suitcase. In certain circumstances we can use it to refer to a living thing, especially if the gender of the thing is not known, such as a pet or a baby. For example, when a baby is born, you might say things such as *It's a boy!* or *It's a girl!* Or, you could use the word *it* to refer to a general situation, as seen in expressions such as *It is raining!* or *It is too hot outside!*

The point here is that in German, the word **es** can be used in many of the same ways as the word *it* can be used in English, so keep this in mind as you translate the exercises.

EXERCISES

1. **Es ist Abend.**
2. **Es ist Nacht.**
3. **Es ist Tag.**
4. **Es ist Morgen.**
5. **Sie ist eine Frau.**
6. **Er ist nicht mein Bruder.**
7. **Er ist ein Mann.**
8. **Guten Abend, mein Freund!**
9. **Guten Tag, Vater!**
10. **Er ist mein Sohn.**

Answers on page 192.

LESSON 48

MORE ABOUT NEGATION

In German, there are two ways to negate a sentence. You already know one way to do it, which uses the word **nicht**. Here's an example of how to use **nicht** in a sentence:

Ich bin nicht der Mann. *(I am not the man.)*

But in German, there is more than one way to negate a sentence. Let's look at that sentence again, this time paying special attention to the word **der**.

Ich bin nicht <u>der</u> Mann. *(I am not <u>the</u> man.)*

In that example, the speaker was saying that he was not *the* something—that is, he was using the definite article. You can also use **nicht** to negate a sentence like this one:

Ich bin nicht <u>dein</u> Bruder. *(I am not <u>your</u> brother.)*

In that sentence, the speaker was saying that he wasn't *your* something—that is, he was using a possessive adjective (*my, your, his, her*, etc.).

So we use **nicht** in sentences that use a definite article or possessive adjective. But if the sentence uses an indefinite article, it's a different story! Observe this sentence:

I am not <u>a</u> father.

Notice that in that sentence there was an indefinite article instead of a definite article or possessive adjective like the previous sentences had. Since you are a native English speaker, you might try to construct the sentence like this:

Ich bin nicht <u>ein</u> Vater.

After all, that is a word-for-word translation from the way we would say it in English, right? But in German, that's not the correct way to say it. In German, if you want to make a sentence with an indefinite article negative, you have to word it like this:

I am no father.

The German word we need to use in a sentence like this one is the word **kein**. **Kein** rhymes with *fine* and *line*. Here's an example of how we would use **kein** in a sentence.

Ich bin kein Vater.

Word for word, that sentence would say *I am no father*. But we translate it into English as *I am not a father*.

So here's a quick recap: if you are saying that you aren't something, with the definite article *the* or with a possessive adjective such as *my* or *your*, you would use **nicht**. And if you're saying you aren't something with the indefinite article *a* or *an*, then you would use the word **kein**.

Pretend that each exercise below is a German sentence. Try to figure out if it's the kind of sentence that would require **nicht** or the kind that would require **kein**.

EXERCISES

1. I am not your father.
2. I am not a father.
3. I am not a farmer.
4. You are not my sister.
5. He is not a salesman.
6. It is not my dog.
7. He is not my brother.
8. It is not a car.
9. We are not athletes.
10. She is not my wife.

Answers on page 192.

LESSON 49

PRACTICING WITH KEIN

In the last lesson, we learned about the German word **kein**. We learned that **kein** is used to negate a sentence with an indefinite article, like this one:

Ich bin kein Vater. *(I am not a father.)*

Literally, a sentence like that says *I am no father*, but we translate it into English as *I am not a father*.

Kein is another **ein** word, so it changes form to agree with the gender of the noun it negates. Observe the forms of **kein** in this chart:

Masculine	Feminine	Neuter	Plural
kein	**keine**	**kein**	**keine**

So if you're saying that you are not a masculine noun, you need **kein**, like this:

Ich bin kein Vater. *(I am not a father.)*

If you're saying that you are not a feminine noun, you need **keine**, like this:

Ich bin keine Mutter. *(I am not a mother.)*

And if you're saying that you are not a neuter noun, you need **kein**, like this:

Ich bin kein Kind. *(I am not a child.)*

Soon, you will learn plural verbs in German, and then you'll need to know the plural form of **kein**, which is **keine**.

EXERCISES

1. **Sie ist keine Mutter.**
2. **Er ist kein Junge.**
3. **Es ist Abend.**
4. **Er ist ein Kind.**
5. **Du bist kein Freund.**
6. **Ich bin nicht dein Sohn.**

7. **Du bist nicht meine Freundin.**
8. **Er ist nicht mein Mann.**
9. **Die Eltern, eine Frau und ein Junge.**
10. **Die Mädchen und eine Frau.**

Answers on page 192.

LESSON 50

NEW WORD   **wir sind**

MEANING   *we are*

PRONUNCIATION TIP: **Wir** starts with a *v* sound and ends with an open *r* sound, so it sounds something like *veeah*. **Sind** sounds like *zint*.

Wir is the pronoun here, and it means *we*. **Sind** is the verb which means *are*.

EXERCISES

1. **Wir sind Kinder.**
2. **Wir sind deine Eltern.**
3. **Wir sind keine Freunde.**
4. **Du bist meine Mutter.**
5. **Sie ist nicht meine Freundin.**
6. **Der Mann ist nicht mein Vater.**
7. **Guten Abend, meine Tochter.**
8. **Ich bin dein Mann.**
9. **Meine Mutter ist meine Freundin.**
10. **Meine Freundinnen und deine Kinder.**

Answers on page 192.

LESSON 51

NEW WORD   **ihr seid**

MEANING   *you are* (plural)

PRONUNCIATION TIP: Pronounce **ihr** with an open *r* sound, like *ee-ah*. **Seid** starts with a *z* sound and ends with a *t* sound, so it sounds something like *zite*.

Ihr is a pronoun that means *you* (plural). **Seid** is the verb.

You already know that **du bist** means *you are*. We use **du bist** when speaking to one person. **Ihr seid** also means *you are*, but with one important difference: **ihr seid** is plural. The English word *you* can refer to one person or more than one person. But other languages such as French, Spanish, and German have a separate word for singular *you* and for plural *you*.

Sometimes English speakers use expressions such as *you all, you guys,* or *you people* to try to make it clear that we are talking to more than one person. In the southeastern United States, we often use the contraction *y'all* to address more than one person (never just one). *Y'all* is simply a contraction of the words *you* and *all*. *Y'all* rhymes with *hall, ball,* and *fall*. So, in the answer key, **ihr seid** will be translated as *y'all are* to help you distinguish plural *you* from singular *you*. If you are from the southeastern United States, using this word will be easy for you. If not, y'all will get used to it after using it a few times. In any case, just try to have fun with it.

EXERCISES

1. **Ihr seid Kinder.**
2. **Ihr seid meine Eltern.**
3. **Ihr seid meine Freunde.**
4. **Guten Tag, mein Freund.**
5. **Wir sind nicht deine Töchter.**
6. **Sie ist meine Freundin.**
7. **Es ist Morgen.**
8. **Du bist kein Junge.**
9. **Er ist mein Bruder.**
10. **Ich bin nicht deine Schwester.**

Answers on page 193.

54

LESSON 52

NEW WORD   **sind**

MEANING   *are*

PRONUNCIATION TIP: **Sind** sounds like *zint*.

You might be thinking to yourself, "Hey, I already know the word **sind**, and I already know that it means *are*." And that's true—but you can use **sind** not only with *we* sentences like this...

> **Wir sind Männer.** *(We are men.)*

...but also with *they* sentences like this:

> **Die Frauen sind meine Schwestern.** *(The women are my sisters.)*

So the German **sind** means *are* as in *we are*, and it means *are* as in *they are*.

EXERCISES

1. **Meine Söhne sind deine Freunde.**
2. **Die Männer sind meine Brüder.**
3. **Die Frauen sind meine Schwestern und meine Frau.**
4. **Ihr seid meine Eltern.**
5. **Die Mädchen sind meine Töchter.**
6. **Wir sind deine Kinder.**
7. **Er ist mein Freund.**
8. **Sie ist meine Frau.**
9. **Es ist Nacht.**
10. **Du bist meine Mutter.**

Answers on page 193.

LESSON 53

NEW WORD   **sie**

MEANING   *they*

PRONUNCIATION TIP: **Sie** sounds like *zee*.

We really aren't trying to confuse you, but…you already know that the word **sie** can mean *she*, but it can also mean *they*. So if the word **sie** can mean two different things, how do you know what it means when you see it? The way to tell the difference is to examine the verb that **sie** goes with. Let's look at some examples:

> **Sie ist meine Schwester.** *(She is my sister.)*

In that example, **sie** means *she*. Notice that the verb is **ist**. If you translated **sie** here as *they*, it wouldn't make any sense because then the sentence would say *They is my sister.* Here's another example.

> **Sie sind meine Eltern.** *(They are my parents.)*

In that example, **sie** means *they*. Notice that the verb is **sind**. If you translated **sie** here as *she*, it wouldn't make any sense because then the sentence would say *She are my parents.*

So, to make a long story short, you will have to use the context to figure out what **sie** means as you translate the exercises. Whenever you see the word **sie**, look at the context and try to figure out if it means *she* or *they*.

EXERCISES

1. **Sie sind meine Schwestern.**
2. **Sie sind meine Freundinnen.**
3. **Sie sind nicht meine Töchter.**
4. **Ihr seid meine Schwestern.**
5. **Wir sind deine Freunde und Brüder.**
6. **Sie ist meine Mutter.**
7. **Du bist kein Junge. Du bist ein Mann.**
8. **Ich bin kein Vater.**
9. **Du bist nicht mein Sohn. Du bist meine Tochter.**
10. **Wir sind nicht deine Kinder. Wir sind deine Eltern.**

Answers on page 193.

56

LESSON 54

TITLES AND NAMES

When talking to other people, we use various names and titles to address them. If you know a person well, you will probably use his or her first name. But if it's a person you don't know very well or someone older than you, you might refer to him or her by a form of address such as *Mr.*, *Mrs.*, or *Miss*.

In English, *Mr.* is a title given to adult men, whether married or not. *Mrs.* is used for married women, *Miss* is used for unmarried women, and *Ms.* can refer to women of any marital status.

If you say **Herr** and then the man's last name, **Herr** just means *Mister*, like in these examples:

- **Guten Tag, Herr Smith.** (*Good day, Mr. Smith.*)
- **Herr Smith ist mein Freund.** (*Mr. Smith is my friend.*)
- **Ich bin Herr Smith.** (*I am Mr. Smith.*)

You already know the word **Frau**, which means *woman*, but as a title it can also mean *Mrs.*, *Miss*, or *Ms.* As a title, the word **Frau** does not refer to any particular marital status. So, if you say **Frau** and then the woman's last name, the word **Frau** could translate into English as *Mrs.*, *Miss*, or *Ms.*, as seen in these examples:

- **Guten Tag, Frau Smith.** (*Good day, Mrs./Miss/Ms. Smith.*)
- **Frau Smith ist meine Freundin.** (*Mrs./Miss/Ms. Smith is my friend.*)
- **Ich bin Frau Smith.** (*I am Mrs./Miss/Ms. Smith.*)

The word **Fräulein** was once used for unmarried women, but this has fallen out of use.

In addition to the titles we mentioned above, we will also put a few first names in the exercises just for practice—so watch for names like Helga, Jürgen, and maybe a few others, too.

1. **Guten Tag, Herr Smith.**
2. **Auf Wiedersehen, Frau Smith.**
3. **Hans ist mein Mann.**
4. **Frau Jones ist nicht meine Schwester.**
5. **Sie sind meine Eltern und deine Kinder.**
6. **Ihr seid meine Freunde.**
7. **Er ist mein Vater und sie ist meine Mutter.**
8. **Es ist Tag.**
9. **Wir sind keine Väter.**
10. **Du bist ein Mädchen und ich bin eine Frau.**

Answers on page 193.

LESSON 55

PERSON

We have already covered singular and plural, so now let's talk about another quality that verbs have. In German, verbs (with help from their pronouns) tell not only what action is taking place, but also who is performing the action. Verbs can be in the first person, second person, or third person.

- ❏ Verbs that refer to *I* or *we* are first person (the person who is speaking).

- ❏ Verbs that refer to *you*, either singular or plural, are second person (the person or people to whom the speaker is speaking). In this book we will use *y'all* for the second person plural to help distinguish it from the second person singular.

- ❏ Verbs that refer to *he, she, it*, or *they* are third person (the person, thing, people, or things being spoken about).

58

The following chart should help illustrate this concept:

	SINGULAR	PLURAL
FIRST PERSON	I	we
SECOND PERSON	you	you
THIRD PERSON	he, she, it	they

y'all

In the exercises below, determine what the subject of each sentence is. Then, determine if it is first person, second person, or third person. Finally, determine whether it is singular or plural.

EXERCISES

1. I am tired.
2. You are really good at chess.
3. She passed the test.
4. We are going to school.
5. Y'all have an expensive car.
6. They eat breakfast at Aunt Martha's house every Saturday.
7. He is a trombone player.
8. It is a history book.
9. Y'all really know how to throw a party.
10. The flowers in your garden are very colorful.

Answers on page 193.

LESSON 56

Now let's put all the German verbs you know into a chart, along with their accompanying pronouns.

	SINGULAR	PLURAL
FIRST PERSON	**ich bin**	**wir sind**
SECOND PERSON	**du bist**	**ihr seid**
THIRD PERSON	**er/sie/es ist**	**sie sind**

As you memorize this chart, don't just memorize the German words—also think about what each word means.

LESSON 57

NEW WORD   **Hund / Katze**

MEANING   *dog / cat*

PRONUNCIATION TIP: The *d* at the end of the word **Hund** sounds like a *t*, so **Hund** sounds something like *hoont*. **Katze** sounds something like *KAHT-suh*.

The word **Hund** is a masculine noun, even when it refers to a female dog. To make it plural, just add the letter *e* to the end, like this:

   Hund ⟶ Hunde

The word **Katze** is a feminine noun, even when it refers to a male cat. To make it plural, add an *n* to the end, like this:

   Katze ⟶ Katzen

EXERCISES

1. **Du bist nicht mein Hund. Du bist meine Katze.**
2. **Die Katze ist meine Freundin.**
3. **Wir sind keine Hunde. Wir sind Katzen.**
4. **Herr Smith ist nicht mein Vater. Er ist mein Bruder.**
5. **Ihr seid meine Hunde.**
6. **Deine Mutter ist meine Schwester.**
7. **Wir sind nicht deine Freunde. Wir sind deine Eltern.**
8. **Sarah ist deine Schwester. Sie ist meine Freundin.**
9. **Herr und Frau Jones sind meine Eltern.**
10. **Sie ist meine Schwester und er ist mein Bruder.**

Answers on page 193.

LESSON 58

NUMBERS

PRONUNCIATION TIP: Some of these numbers will sound unusual to your English-speaking ears, so listen carefully to the pronunciation recordings.

In this lesson, let's try to memorize the numbers *one* through *six* in German. Here is a chart to help you learn these numbers.

ENGLISH	GERMAN
zero	**null**
one	**eins**
two	**zwei**
three	**drei**
four	**vier**
five	**fünf**
six	**sechs**

Notice that the word for the number *one* is **eins**, but this is only for counting. When you say *one* before a noun, you must use the indefinite article, which is either **ein**, **eine**, or **ein,** depending on the gender of the noun.

EXERCISES

1. **Ein Mann.**
2. **Zwei Frauen, drei Kinder, vier Katzen und fünf Hunde.**
3. **356-0142 (drei fünf sechs null eins vier zwei).**
4. **Zwei Jungen und fünf Frauen.**
5. **Sechs Hunde und vier Katzen.**
6. **Sie sind meine Töchter.**
7. **Wir sind nicht deine Eltern.**
8. **Ihr seid meine Brüder.**
9. **Herr Smith ist mein Vater. Helga ist meine Schwester.**
10. **Du bist kein Kind.**

Answers on page 193.

LESSON 59

NUMBERS, CONTINUED

PRONUNCIATION TIP: Remember to listen carefully to the pronunciation recordings.

In this lesson, let's try to memorize the numbers *seven* through *twelve* in German. Here is a chart to help you learn these numbers.

English	German
seven	**sieben**
eight	**acht**
nine	**neun**
ten	**zehn**
eleven	**elf**
twelve	**zwölf**

EXERCISES

1. **Sieben Freunde.**
2. **Neun Jungen und zwölf Mädchen.**
3. **790-8415 (sieben neun null acht vier eins fünf).**
4. **Zehn Hunde und zwölf Katzen.**
5. **Die Frau ist meine Freundin. Arnold ist mein Bruder.**
6. **Ich bin deine Schwester und du bist mein Bruder.**
7. **Sie ist nicht deine Freundin.**
8. **Frau Smith ist nicht meine Schwester. Sie ist meine Mutter.**
9. **Sie sind nicht meine Kinder.**
10. **Wir sind die Eltern und ihr seid die Kinder.**

Answers on page 194.

LESSON 60

NEW WORD   **Stuhl**

MEANING   *chair*

PRONUNCIATION TIP: The *s* at the beginning of **Stuhl** sounds like the *sh* in *shout.*

The word **Stuhl** is masculine.

To make **Stuhl** plural, we change both the vowel sound and the ending. The vowel sound changes to a rounded *ü* (notice the **Umlaut** over the letter *u*). Also, the letter *e* gets added to the end.

Stuhl ⟶ Stühle

When you say **Stühle**, round your lips. It sounds something like *SHTEWL-uh* or *SHTEEL-uh.* When you add an *e* to **Stuhl** to make it plural, it gives the word an additional syllable.

EXERCISES

1. **Der Stuhl.**
2. **Neun Kinder und acht Stühle!**
3. **Elf Katzen und sieben Hunde.**
4. **Zwei Schwestern und sechs Brüder.**
5. **Fünf Katzen und drei Hunde.**
6. **Wir sind keine Hunde. Wir sind Katzen.**
7. **Herr Jones ist nicht mein Bruder. Er ist mein Sohn.**
8. **Du bist mein Freund.**
9. **Die Männer sind meine Brüder.**
10. **Guten Tag, Jürgen.**

Answers on page 194.

LESSON 61

NEW WORD   **Tisch**

MEANING   *table*

PRONUNCIATION TIP: **Tisch** sounds just like it looks—like *tish*.

Tisch is a masculine noun. To form the plural, add the letter *e*, like this:

Tisch   ⟶   Tische

When you add an *e* to **Tisch** to make it plural, it gives the word an additional syllable. So **Tische** sounds something like *TISH-uh*.

EXERCISES

1. **Elf Tische und acht Stühle.**
2. **Fünf Stühle und sieben Tische.**
3. **Eine Katze und neun Hunde.**
4. **Der Tisch und ein Stuhl.**
5. **Guten Tag, Sarah.**
6. **Ihr seid Katzen. Ihr seid keine Hunde.**
7. **Es ist kein Tisch. Es ist ein Stuhl.**
8. **Sie ist meine Schwester. Er ist mein Bruder.**
9. **Der Mann und die Frau sind meine Eltern.**
10. **Die Jungen sind meine Söhne.**

Answers on page 194.

LESSON 62

DIRECT OBJECTS

A direct object is a noun that is the target of the action being performed by the subject of the sentence. Here is an example:

> Harold plays the drums.

In this sentence, the word *drums* is the direct object. Here is another example:

> Helen ate the orange.

In this sentence, the word *orange* is the direct object. See if you can find the direct object in each of the exercises below:

EXERCISES

1. Mr. Jones bought a newspaper.
2. I will see a movie tomorrow.
3. Harry is playing the trombone.
4. On Saturday, we will play baseball.
5. James caught a fish.
6. They accidentally broke the radio.
7. Y'all painted the wrong building.
8. Yesterday we listened to a long speech.
9. Mr. Underwood lost his wallet.
10. Geraldine saw a deer in the woods.

Answers on page 194.

LESSON 63

THE PREDICATE NOMINATIVE

In the last lesson, you learned that a direct object is the target of the action. For example, in the following sentence the word *dog* is the direct object.

Fred chased the dog.

But what if the verb is not an action verb? What if the verb is a verb of being or existing, as in this example:

Fred is a dog.

In that sentence, the word *dog* is not a direct object. Why? Because only an action verb can generate a direct object. The verb in that sentence is the word *is*, which is a verb of being. When you use a verb of being to make a "this is that" kind of sentence, the "that" word is not a direct object—instead, it is called a *predicate nominative*. Therefore in the sentence above, the word *dog* is a *predicate nominative*.

In each of the following exercises the word *dog* is either a direct object or a predicate nominative. See if you can figure out which one it is.

EXERCISES

1. Fluffy is our dog.
2. The cat chased the dog.
3. We saw the dog.
4. Did you feed the dog?
5. The kids are petting the dog.
6. A golden retriever is a dog.
7. Yesterday we bathed the dog.
8. The vet examined the dog.
9. Rex was our dog.
10. My cat sees the dog.

Answers on page 194.

LESSON 64

THE DEFINITE ARTICLE AND DIRECT OBJECTS

You now have some experience working with the definite article **der**. You already know that **der** changes its form depending on whether it is masculine, feminine, or neuter. But here in this lesson, it's time to learn about the fact that the definite article can change form not only for gender, but for the role it plays in a sentence.

One situation in which the definite article will change is when it introduces a direct object that is masculine and singular. When this happens, the definite article becomes **den** instead of **der**. **Den** rhymes with *lane* and *main*. Let's compare some sentences so we can observe how this works in German.

> The dog is in the backyard.

In this sentence, the word *dog* is the subject. So if this were a German sentence, you would use **der**, like this:

> **Der** dog is in the backyard.

But what about this sentence:

> I see the dog.

In this sentence, the word *dog* is not the subject—it is the direct object. So if this sentence were in German, you wouldn't put **der** in front of the word *dog*—you would put **den**, like this:

> I see **den** dog.

Again, this change is only for masculine singular nouns. When a feminine noun, neuter noun, or plural noun is a direct object, the definite article stays the same as it would normally be when it is the subject.

Also if a noun is a predicate nominative, it keeps the same article as when it's the subject. So in this sentence…

> Rex is the dog.

…the word *dog* is a predicate nominative, not a direct object, so it still gets the same article as if it were the subject, like this:

Rex is **der** dog.

In the exercises below, choose as your answer either **der** or **den**. Then, give the reason for your choice. Choose from among the following three reasons:

- Because it is the subject of the sentence
- Because it is the direct object of the sentence
- Because it is a predicate nominative

Write your answers in your notebook or on a separate sheet of paper.

EXERCISES

1. I have (**der/den**) dog.   *den*
2. He is (**der/den**) dog.   *der*
3. (**Der/Den**) dog is large.   *Der*
4. They see (**der/den**) dog.   *den*
5. Fluffy is (**der/den**) dog.   *den   der*
6. Jane is feeding (**der/den**) dog.   *der   den*
7. That large animal over there is (**der/den**) dog.   *der*
8. (**Der/Den**) dog ran through our yard.   *der*
9. We forgot to walk (**der/den**) dog!   *den*
10. Rex is (**der/den**) dog.   *der*

Answers on page 194.

LESSON 65

EIN-WORDS WITH DIRECT OBJECTS

In the last lesson we learned that when a masculine singular noun is a direct object, the definite article changes from **der** to **den**. In this lesson we want to show you that **ein** words go through a similar change when they come before a masculine singular direct object. Just for review, the **ein** words you know so far are **ein**, **mein**, **dein**, and **kein**.

Here's the change: when an **ein** word is used before a masculine singular noun that is a direct object, we change the ending by adding *-en*.

- **ein** ⟶ **einen**

- **kein** ⟶ **keinen**

- **mein** ⟶ **meinen**

- **dein** ⟶ **deinen**

And the pattern will be the same for whatever other **ein** words you learn in the future. Here's a sentence we can work with to practice using these new forms in a sentence:

> I have a dog.

In that sentence the word *dog* is the direct object—so if it were a German sentence you would need to use **einen**, like this:

> I have **einen** dog.

Here's another example:

> We do not have a dog.

In German, that kind of sentence would be worded like this:

> We have no dog.

In that sentence, *dog*, again, is a masculine singular noun and it is the direct object—if it were a German sentence you would need to use **keinen**, like this:

We have **keinen** dog.

Again, this change is only for masculine singular nouns. When a feminine, neuter noun, or plural noun is a direct object, the **ein** word stays the same as would normally be when it is part of the subject.

Also if a noun is a predicate nominative, it keeps the same article as when it's the subject. Observe this sentence:

Rex is a dog.

Here the word *dog* is a predicate nominative, not a direct object, so it still gets the same **ein** word as if it were the subject, like this:

Rex is **ein** dog.

So just for practice, let's do the same thing we did in the last lesson, only with **ein** words. In the exercises below, choose the correct form of the word. Then, give the reason for your choice. Choose from among the following three reasons:

- Because it is the subject of the sentence
- Because it is the direct object of the sentence
- Because it is a predicate nominative

Write your answers in your notebook or on a separate sheet of paper.

EXERCISES

1. We have (**ein/einen**) dog.
2. Fluffy is (**mein/meinen**) dog.
3. (**Dein/Deinen**) dog is in the backyard.
4. Spot is not (**mein/meinen**) dog.
5. We have (**kein/keinen**) dog.
6. My daughter wants (**ein/einen**) dog.
7. That is (**kein/keinen**) dog.
8. (**Ein/einen**) dog is in the yard.
9. I see (**dein/deinen**) dog.
10. I need to walk (**mein/meinen**) dog.

Answers on page 194.

ESSON 66

NEW WORD   **ich habe**

MEANING   *I have*

PR̶O̶.̶   ̶IO̶N̶ TIP: The *ch* in **ich** is a whooshing sound.

This lesson is special because here you are learning your first action verb in German. All the verbs you have learned so far have been verbs of being or existing—but now that we know an action verb, we can make more complex German sentences with direct objects.

Since these sentences have direct objects, watch out for masculine singular direct objects—when you see those, you will see forms that end with *-en*, like **den**, **einen**, **keinen**, etc.

EXERCISES

1. **Ich habe den Hund.**
2. **Ich habe eine Tochter.**
3. **Ich habe den Stuhl.**
4. **Ich habe keinen Stuhl.**
5. **Ich habe keinen Mann.**
6. **Sie sind meine Freunde.**
7. **Ich habe einen Sohn und eine Tochter.**
8. **Ich bin deine Mutter.**
9. **Ihr seid meine Freundinnen.**
10. **Ich habe einen Hund.**

Answers on page 195.

LESSON 67

WORD ORDER WITH "NICHT" AND "KEIN"

In German, the order of words in a sentence is a big deal. You can't put German words in whatever order you want—instead, there is a particular order that they should go in, depending on what kind of sentence it is.

Recently, you have learned about action verbs, direct objects, and predicate nominatives. And since you are learning how to make more complicated sentences with direct objects, you need to learn more about the order the words should follow in this kind of sentence. In this particular lesson we will examine where **nicht** and **kein** should be placed in the structure of the sentence.

If a direct object has a definite article or possessive adjective, you must negate the sentence with **nicht**, and you must put **nicht** *after* the direct object. Here are some examples:

- **Ich habe den Stuhl nicht.** *(I do not have the chair.)*
- **Ich habe deinen Stuhl nicht.** *(I do not have your chair.)*

If a direct object has an indefinite article, you must negate the sentence with **kein**, and you must put **kein** *before* the direct object (this is the same as when you use **kein** with a predicate nominative).

> **Ich habe keinen Stuhl.** *(I have no chair.)*

That sentence literally says *I have no chair*, but we translate it into English as *I do not have a chair.*

Again, word order is a big deal in German, so as you continue forward in your studies, pay attention to where you put each word in relation to the other words in the sentence.

EXERCISES

1. **Ich habe eine Frau.**
2. **Ich habe keine Tochter.**
3. **Ich habe den Stuhl nicht.**
4. **Ich habe deinen Hund nicht.**

5. **Ich habe eine Katze.**
6. **Du bist nicht mein Freund.**
7. **Ihr seid meine Eltern.**
8. **Ich bin dein Vater.**
9. **Ich habe keine Töchter.**
10. **Ich habe eine Katze.**

Answers on page 195.

LESSON 68

NEW WORD **Auto**

MEANING *car*

The word **Auto** is an example of one of the many words which the German language has borrowed from other languages. We call these borrowed words *loan words*. Like most loan words in German, **Auto** is neuter in gender, so it needs a neuter article like **das** or **ein**.

Auto becomes plural by adding an *s*, like this:

Auto ⟶ Autos

EXERCISES
1. **Ich habe ein Auto.**
2. **Ich habe dein Auto nicht.**
3. **Ich habe zwei Kinder, drei Katzen und einen Hund.**
4. **Ich habe sieben Schwestern und acht Brüder.**
5. **Du bist meine Tochter. Ich bin dein Vater.**
6. **Ich habe keinen Stuhl.**
7. **Wir sind Brüder und Schwestern.**
8. **Ich habe deinen Hund.**
9. **Ihr seid meine Freunde.**
10. **Ich habe eine Katze und einen Hund.**

Answers on page 195.

LESSON 69

NEW WORD   **du hast**

MEANING   *you have*

This chart should come in handy as we learn all the different forms of **ich habe**.

	SINGULAR	PLURAL
FIRST PERSON	**ich habe**	
SECOND PERSON	**du hast**	
THIRD PERSON		

EXERCISES

1. **Du hast ein Auto und ich habe zwei Autos.**
2. **Du hast einen Tisch.**
3. **Ich habe den Hund. Ich habe die Katze nicht.**
4. **Du hast drei Schwestern und fünf Brüder.**
5. **Du hast zehn Katzen und drei Hunde.**
6. **Er ist nicht mein Vater. Er ist Herr Johnson.**
7. **Du bist meine Freundin. Wir sind Freundinnen.**
8. **Du hast keine Kinder.**
9. **Sie ist eine Katze. Sie ist kein Hund!**
10. **Du hast keinen Stuhl.**

Answers on page 195.

LESSON 70

NEW WORD   **er / sie / es hat**

MEANING   *he / she / it has*

The chart is now halfway full.

	SINGULAR	PLURAL
FIRST PERSON	**ich habe**	
SECOND PERSON	**du hast**	
THIRD PERSON	**er/sie/es hat**	

EXERCISES

1. **Sie hat einen Hund.**
2. **Das Kind hat keine Katze. Es hat einen Hund.**
3. **Du hast einen Tisch und zwei Stühle.**
4. **Meine Tochter hat mein Auto.**
5. **Er hat neun Kinder—zwei Söhne und sieben Töchter.**
6. **Ich bin dein Freund.**
7. **Du hast zehn Schwestern und einen Bruder.**
8. **Wir sind nicht deine Eltern.**
9. **Sie sind meine Freunde und ihr seid meine Brüder.**
10. **Arnold hat den Hund.**

Answers on page 195.

LESSON 71

NEW WORD **aber**

MEANING *but*

Aber means *but.* You can use it just as you would use the conjunction *but* in English. Here's an example:

Ich habe eine Katze, aber du hast einen Hund. *(I have a cat, but you have a dog.)*

EXERCISES

1. **Ich habe keinen Hund, aber meine Mutter hat einen Hund.**
2. **Du hast keine Katze, aber dein Freund hat eine Katze.**
3. **Meine Katze ist meine Freundin und dein Hund ist dein Freund.**
4. **Mein Bruder hat mein Auto.**
5. **Ich habe vier Hunde und fünf Katzen.**
6. **Frau Smith hat deinen Hund.**
7. **Sonja ist meine Freundin, aber Peter ist nicht mein Freund.**
8. **Du hast sechs Kinder, aber ich habe neun Kinder.**
9. **Mein Sohn hat eine Katze und einen Hund.**
10. **Er hat drei Stühle, aber ich habe den Tisch.**

Answers on page 195.

LESSON 72

NEW WORD   **wir haben**

MEANING   *we have*

We're halfway there!

	SINGULAR	PLURAL
FIRST PERSON	**ich habe**	**wir haben**
SECOND PERSON	**du hast**	
THIRD PERSON	**er/sie/es hat**	

EXERCISES

1. **Wir haben kein Auto, aber du hast fünf Autos.**
2. **Wir haben keinen Bruder, aber wir haben drei Schwestern.**
3. **Wir haben einen Hund, aber wir haben keine Katze.**
4. **Meine Frau hat das Auto.**
5. **Ich habe deinen Hund nicht.**
6. **Die Mädchen sind meine Schwestern und die Jungen sind meine Brüder.**
7. **Sie hat einen Sohn und fünf Töchter.**
8. **Wir haben keinen Sohn, aber wir haben eine Tochter.**
9. **Herr Jones hat keine Frau, aber er hat acht Schwestern.**
10. **Du bist meine Schwester, aber du bist nicht meine Freundin.**

Answers on page 195.

LESSON 73

NEW WORD   **ihr habt**

MEANING   *y'all have*

PRONUNCIATION TIP: The *b* in **habt** sounds like a *p*, so **habt** sounds something like *hopped*.

	SINGULAR	PLURAL
FIRST PERSON	ich habe	wir haben
SECOND PERSON	du hast	ihr habt
THIRD PERSON	er/sie/es hat	

EXERCISES

1. **Ihr habt mein Auto.**
2. **Ihr habt meinen Hund und meine Katze.**
3. **Ihr habt elf Kinder, aber wir haben keine Kinder.**
4. **Der Junge hat meinen Hund.**
5. **Das Mädchen hat keinen Hund.**
6. **Du hast keine Schwestern, aber ich habe zwölf Schwestern und einen Bruder.**
7. **Meine Schwester hat den Stuhl.**
8. **Sie sind meine Kinder.**
9. **Die Kinder sind deine Brüder und deine Schwestern.**
10. **Sie ist nicht meine Freundin. Sie ist meine Frau.**

Answers on page 196.

79

LESSON 74

NEW WORD   **sie haben**

MEANING   *they have*

	SINGULAR	PLURAL
FIRST PERSON	**ich habe**	**wir haben**
SECOND PERSON	**du hast**	**ihr habt**
THIRD PERSON	**er/sie/es hat**	**sie haben**

Remember that the word **sie** can mean either *she* or *they*. To figure out which one it is, just look at the verb that goes with it. Let's look at some examples:

Sie hat einen Hund. *(She has a dog.)*

In this example you know that **sie** means *she* because it has the verb **hat** with it. If **sie** meant *they*, it wouldn't make any sense because it would say *they has a dog*. Here's another example:

Sie haben einen Hund. *(They have a dog.)*

In that example, you know that **sie** means *they* because it has the verb **haben**. If **sie** meant *she*, it wouldn't make any sense because it would say *she have a dog*.

So use context and it will be clear which is which. In the exercises below, when you see the word **sie**, try to figure out if it means *she* or *they*.

EXERCISES

1. **Sie hat mein Auto!**
2. **Sie haben keinen Hund, aber wir haben sechs Hunde.**
3. **Ihr habt keinen Hund.**
4. **Ich habe vier Katzen und acht Hunde.**
5. **Die Jungen sind meine Söhne und das Mädchen ist meine Tochter.**
6. **Meine Brüder haben mein Auto.**
7. **Herr Smith hat sechs Brüder, aber ich habe keinen Bruder.**

8. **Du hast einen Hund und eine Katze.**
9. **Meine Schwester hat einen Hund, aber meine Mutter hat eine Katze.**
10. **Wir haben kein Auto, aber du hast fünf Autos.**

Answers on page 196.

LESSON 75

REVIEW

We now know all the present tense forms of **ich bin** and **ich habe**. Let's review them now. Here is the chart for **ich bin**:

	SINGULAR	PLURAL
FIRST PERSON	**ich bin**	**wir sind**
SECOND PERSON	**du bist**	**ihr seid**
THIRD PERSON	**er/sie/es ist**	**sie sind**

You should make every effort to memorize these forms. Chant them. Sing them. Do whatever helps you to memorize the different verb forms. Here is the chart for **ich habe**:

	SINGULAR	PLURAL
FIRST PERSON	**ich habe**	**wir haben**
SECOND PERSON	**du hast**	**ihr habt**
THIRD PERSON	**er/sie/es hat**	**sie haben**

As you repeat or recite these verb forms, try to think of what each word means as you say it.

LESSON 76

NEW WORD   **auch**

MEANING   *also, too*

PRONUNCIATION TIP: **Auch** sounds like the *ow* in *clown*, but with a scraping sound at the end.

Auch can also mean *even* as in the sentence *Even the dog would not eat it.* But in this book, we will just use **auch** to mean *also* or *too*.

EXERCISES

1. **Wir haben einen Hund. Dieter und Nina haben auch einen Hund.**
2. **Ich habe einen Sohn. Meine Freundin Natascha hat auch einen Sohn.**
3. **Sie hat acht Katzen und zehn Hunde.**
4. **Mein Hund ist mein Freund.**
5. **Du hast vier Töchter, aber ich habe sieben Töchter.**
6. **Simon hat eine Schwester, aber er hat keinen Bruder.**
7. **Sie ist meine Mutter.**
8. **Du hast eine Mutter und einen Vater. Sie sind deine Eltern.**
9. **Ich bin eine Frau und du bist ein Mann.**
10. **Sie haben fünf Autos, aber ihr habt kein Auto.**

Answers on page 196.

LESSON 77

CASES

In German, articles and adjectives change according to what role or function they play in a given sentence. These different roles or functions are called *cases*. When we use a word as the subject of a sentence, that word is said to be in the *nominative case*. We also use the nominative case for predicate nominatives. When we use a word as a direct object, that word is said to be in the *accusative case*. There are four cases in all.

In the chart below, observe the forms of the definite article. Notice that the nominative forms are the same as the the accusative forms, except for the masculine gender. In the masculine gender, **der** changes to **den** in the accusative case—that is, when it is a direct object. To help draw your attention to his important point, we have circled this form in the chart below.

	MASCULINE	FEMININE	NEUTER	PLURAL
NOMINATIVE (SUBJ./PRED. NOM.)	der	die	das	die
ACCUSATIVE (DIRECT OBJECT)	(den)	die	das	die

Ein words follow this same pattern. The nominative forms are the same as the accusative forms except for the masculine gender. In the masculine gender, the ending changes to *-en* in the accusative case—that is, when it is a direct object. That particular form is circled in the chart below, in which **mein** is used to show the various forms.

	MASCULINE	FEMININE	NEUTER	PLURAL
NOMINATIVE (SUBJ./PRED. NOM.)	mein	meine	mein	meine
ACCUSATIVE (DIRECT OBJECT)	(meinen)	meine	mein	meine

Each case performs certain functions while working together with the other cases to create meaningful sentences. As you can see from the chart, you already have experience working with two of the four cases. As you learn the third and fourth cases, you will be able to translate more complex (and interesting) exercises.

LESSON 78

AGREEMENT

In German, words work together to create meaningful sentences. One important concept to understand about the way words work together is called *agreement*. When we talk about agreement, what we mean is that there are certain situations in which two words must have the same case, the same number, or the same gender. Let's learn more about agreement by studying some of the specific situations in which words must agree with each other.

CASE

A noun and its article must be in the same case. Observe the following sentence.

Ich bin der Mann.

Der and **Mann** are both nominative, so they agree and the sentence makes sense. But what about this sentence:

Ich bin den Mann.

This sentence doesn't make any sense because **den** is an accusative article and **Mann** is supposed to be nominative. Call the grammar police!

NUMBER

A noun and its article must both be either singular or plural. In the example sentence below, notice that **der** and **Mann** are both singular.

Ich bin der Mann.

Der and **Mann** are both singular, so they agree and the sentence makes sense. But what about this sentence:

Ich bin der Männer.

This sentence doesn't make any sense because **der** is singular and **Männer** is plural. What a mess!

GENDER

A noun and its article must both be the same gender. In the example sentence below, notice that **das** and **Mädchen** are both neuter.

Das Mädchen ist meine Schwester.

Das and **Mädchen** are both neuter, so they agree and the sentence makes sense. But what about this sentence:

Der Mädchen ist meine Schwester.

This sentence doesn't make any sense because **der** is masculine and **Mädchen** is neuter. Grammar fail!

SUBJECT AND VERB

When it comes to verbs, we have two variables to think about: person and number. A verb can be first person, second person, or third person. Also, a verb can be singular or plural. In a sentence, the subject must be in the same person and number as the verb, like this:

Wir sind.

In this sentence, **wir**, the subject, is first person plural. The verb, **sind**, is also first person plural. Therefore, the subject and verb agree, and the sentence makes sense. But what about this sentence:

Wir ist.

This sentence doesn't make any sense because **wir** is first person plural, but **ist** is third person singular. That would be like saying *we is* in English.

PRONOUN AND ANTECEDENT

A pronoun is a word that takes the place of a noun. If a pronoun refers back to a noun already mentioned, that noun is called the *antecedent*. When you use a pronoun, the pronoun must be the same gender as its antecedent. Here's a sentence to help illustrate what we mean:

The <u>girl</u> is thirsty but <u>she</u> has no water.

In this sentence, the word *girl* is the antecedent and the word *she* is the pronoun. In English, the word *girl* is feminine—so when we use a pronoun to take its place, we select the feminine pronoun *she*. Now let's observe that exact same sentence, but in German (**Wasser** is the German word for *water*):

Das <u>Mädchen</u> hat Durst, aber <u>es</u> hat kein Wasser.

In this sentence, **Mädchen** is the antecedent and **es** is the pronoun. The word **Mädchen** is grammatically neuter, so the pronoun must also be neuter. Therefore we have to select the neuter pronoun **es**. As a result, the antecedent and pronoun agree, and the sentence is correct. But what about this sentence:

Das <u>Mädchen</u> hat Durst, aber <u>sie</u> hat kein Wasser.

The sentence above might seem to be correct at first glance because **sie** means *she*, and according to natural gender, a girl is feminine, right? But really this sentence is grammatically incorrect because the feminine pronoun **sie** refers back to the neuter noun **Mädchen**. Even though this kind of sentence is technically incorrect, you may hear German speakers say that kind of thing, trying to mentally match the gender of the pronoun with natural gender instead of grammatical gender.

Our goal in writing this lesson is to raise your awareness of the realities of German grammar (and English grammar, for that matter). Take a moment to think about the material in this lesson. The grammatical concepts presented here are rather important, so if you feel that you don't really understand them, go back and review the lesson again until you get the idea. You'll never outgrow these concepts—as long as you continue studying German, you will need to keep these rules in mind.

LESSON 79

NEW WORD   **Geld**

MEANING   *money*

PRONUNCIATION TIP: **Geld** sounds something like *gelt.*

Geld is neuter, so it needs a neuter article such as **das** or **ein**.

And since we are talking about money, let's learn the German names for a couple of different currencies. In German, the way to say *dollar* (like an American dollar) is **Dollar**. It is a masculine noun, and its plural form is the same as its singular form. Here's an example:

    Ich habe fünf Dollar. *(I have five dollars.)*

And the German way to say *euro* is **Euro**. **Euro** is a masculine noun, and like the word **Dollar**, its plural form is the same as its singular form. It is also masculine.

    Ich habe sieben Euro. *(I have seven euros.)*

EXERCISES

1. **Er hat mein Geld!**
2. **Wir haben Geld—sechs Euro und zwölf Dollar.**
3. **Mein Vater hat kein Geld.**
4. **Der Junge hat acht Dollar.**
5. **Meine Schwestern haben mein Geld.**
6. **Mein Bruder hat Geld, aber ich habe kein Geld.**
7. **Du hast kein Geld, aber ich habe fünf Euro.**
8. **Ihr habt zehn Dollar, aber wir haben kein Geld.**
9. **Sie haben Geld—fünf Euro und zwei Dollar.**
10. **Dein Bruder hat kein Geld, aber deine Schwester hat zehn Dollar.**

Answers on page 196.

LESSON 80

NEW WORD   **sein**

MEANING   *his*

Sein is a possessive adjective that means *his*. It is an **ein** word just like **mein**, **dein**, and **kein**. **Sein** must match the noun it goes with in case, number, and gender.

	MASCULINE	FEMININE	NEUTER	PLURAL
NOMINATIVE (SUBJ./PRED. NOM.)	**sein**	**seine**	**sein**	**seine**
ACCUSATIVE (DIRECT OBJECT)	**seinen**	**seine**	**sein**	**seine**

Notice that like all **ein** words, the nominative and accusative forms are the same, except for the masculine singular form, which ends in *-en*. This form is circled in the chart.

Before we move on to the exercises, we would like to talk a little bit about how context can help you interpret the word **sein**. Observe this sentence:

> Mr. Jones has <u>his</u> dog.

In the above sentence, who does the dog belong to? Is the dog Mr. Jones' own dog? Or maybe somebody else's dog? Who, exactly, is the word *his* referring to? Read this next example, and see if it is more clear about who the dog belongs to.

> It's Bring Your Pet Day at the park. Mr. Smith has his cat, Mr. Johnson has his parrot, and Mr. Jones has <u>his</u> dog.

In that example, the first sentence sets up the context of the situation. In other words, it told us enough context that when we got to the part about *Mr. Jones has his dog*, we knew that the dog belonged to Mr. Jones, not someone else. Now compare that with this next example:

> Mr. Underwood is going on a long trip, so he asked his friends to let his various pets live with them while he is traveling. Mr. Smith has his cat, Mr. Johnson has his parrot, and Mr. Jones has <u>his</u> dog.

In this example, the second sentence is exactly the same as it was before—but the first sentence is different. Here, because of the context, when we got to the part about *Mr. Jones has his dog*, we knew that the dog doesn't really belong to Mr. Jones, but to his friend, Mr. Underwood.

So here's the point: the English word *his* can refer to more than one person, so you must use the context to understand who the word *his* is referring to. And it's the same way in German.

EXERCISES
1. **Mein Vater hat seinen Hund.**
2. **Mein Bruder hat seine Katzen.**
3. **Er hat sein Geld.**
4. **Herr Jones hat sein Auto, aber du hast dein Auto nicht.**
5. **Sie hat neun Dollar, aber ich habe kein Geld.**
6. **Sie haben sieben Dollar und zwei Euro.**
7. **Ich habe zehn Euro, aber meine Freundin hat kein Geld.**
8. **Wir haben einen Hund, aber ihr habt Katzen.**
9. **Sie hat zwei Autos, aber sie hat kein Geld.**
10. **Die Kinder haben den Hund.**

Answers on page 196.

LESSON 81

MORE ABOUT IHR

Sooo...we really aren't trying to confuse you but...you already know the word **ihr** as a pronoun which means *y'all*. But the word **ihr** can also be a possessive adjective which means *her* as in *her car* or *her book*.

The other **ein** words you have studied all have the word **ein** embedded in them: **mein**, **dein**, **kein**, and **sein**. But **ihr** is also an **ein** word, even though it doesn't look like one. Even though it doesn't have the word **ein** embedded in it, it still has the same endings as the other **ein** words, as you can see in the chart below:

	MASCULINE	FEMININE	NEUTER	PLURAL
NOMINATIVE (SUBJ./PRED. NOM.)	ihr	ihre	ihr	ihre
ACCUSATIVE (DIRECT OBJECT)	ihren	ihre	ihr	ihre

And like all **ein** words, the nominative and accusative forms are the same, except for the masculine singular form, which ends in *-en*. This form is circled in the chart.

In the last lesson, we talked at length about how the context can help you interpret the word **sein**. Well, the same thing is true with **ihr**. Use context to determine who the word **ihr** is referring to.

Furthermore, you'll need to use the context to figure out if **ihr** means *y'all* or *her*, as in the following example sentences:

- **Ihr seid Brüder.** *(Y'all are brothers.)*
- **Sie haben ihr Auto.** *(They have her car.)*

In the first example, it was clear that **ihr** meant *y'all* because **ihr** was being used along with the verb **seid**. In the second example, you could tell that **ihr** meant *her* because it was accompanying the word **Auto**. So pay attention, and the context will guide you to the right meaning.

EXERCISES

1. **Meine Mutter hat ihren Hund.**
2. **Meine Schwester hat ihre Katzen.**
3. **Sie hat ihr Geld, aber ihr habt kein Geld.**
4. **Frau Jones hat ein Auto. Ihre Freundin hat auch ein Auto.**
5. **Mein Bruder hat einen Hund.**
6. **Ihr Vater hat ein Auto, aber wir haben kein Auto.**
7. **Ihre Mutter hat sieben Katzen und einen Hund.**
8. **Das Mädchen hat einen Hund, aber es hat keine Katze.**
9. **Herr Smith hat vier Katzen und einen Hund.**
10. **Er hat ein Auto, aber ich habe kein Auto.**

Answers on page 196.

LESSON 82

MORE ABOUT SEIN

You already know that **sein** means *his* and **ihr** means *her*. If a thing belongs to a male, you say it's **sein** thing, and if a thing belongs to a female, you say it's **ihr** thing. Simple, right?

But what if something belongs to a **Mädchen**? Grammatically, the word **Mädchen** is neuter. Or what if something belongs to an inanimate object? Is there a way to say *its* in German? Yes, there is. Observe the chart below.

MASCULINE	FEMININE	NEUTER
sein	ihr	sein

The confusing thing here is that the masculine word **sein** *(his)* and the neuter word **sein** *(its)* are the same word in German. In English, we have the luxury of having different adjectives for *his*, *her*, and *its*. But in German, the masculine and neuter are the same.

So, if you want to say that something belongs to something or someone neuter, you have to use the neuter word **sein**. The forms of neuter **sein** are the same as the forms of masculine **sein**. Here's a chart for the sake of reference.

	MASCULINE	FEMININE	NEUTER	PLURAL
NOMINATIVE (SUBJ./PRED. NOM.)	sein	seine	sein	seine
ACCUSATIVE (DIRECT OBJECT)	seinen	seine	sein	seine

Let's say for example you wanted to say *The girl has her book* in German. Since **Mädchen** is grammatically neuter, you would use the neuter possessive adjective **sein**, like this:

Das Mädchen hat <u>sein</u> Geld.

91

According to natural gender, a girl is feminine. But don't use the feminine **ihr**, like this:

Das Mädchen hat <u>ihr</u> Geld.

That would be incorrect since **Mädchen** is neuter and **ihr** is feminine.

AMBIGUITY WITH "SEIN"

We should point out one other thing about the word **sein**, especially as it interacts with the neuter noun **Mädchen**. Notice that the sentence we showed you above could be translated two ways. Here's that sentence again:

Das Mädchen hat <u>sein</u> Geld.

Since the word **sein** could be either masculine or neuter, you need to be mindful of how it could be translated into English. You could translate **sein** as *his*, and your English translation would be *The girl has his money*. Or, because **sein** can be neuter, it could be referring back to the neuter noun **Mädchen**. In that case, since a girl is feminine in English, you would need to translate it as *her*. Then your translation would read like this: *The girl has her money*. This sentence would mean that the girl has her own money, not somebody else's money.

Therefore in the answer key, for a sentence like that, we will put the answer as *The girl has his/her money*. That way, you can keep in mind the ambiguity of the sentence, remembering that in a short sentence like that, without much context, it is not clear who **sein** is referring to.

EXERCISES

1. **Das Mädchen hat sein Geld.**
2. **Die Jungen haben ihr Geld.**
3. **Die Frau hat ihren Hund.**
4. **Meine Schwester hat ihren Hund, aber sie hat ihre Katze nicht.**
5. **Wir haben kein Auto, aber sie haben drei Autos.**
6. **Ich habe eine Katze. Mein Freund hat auch eine Katze.**
7. **Du hast kein Geld, aber dein Vater hat Geld.**
8. **Ihr seid meine Schwestern und sie sind meine Brüder.**
9. **Meine Schwester hat sieben Dollar.**
10. **Ihr Bruder hat zwei Autos, aber er hat kein Geld.**

Answers on page 197.

LESSON 83

NEW WORD   **Buch / Zeitung**

MEANING   *book / newspaper*

PRONUNCIATION TIP: At the end of the word **Buch**, make a scraping sound at the back of your mouth.

Buch is neuter, so it requires a neuter article such as **das** or **ein**. To make **Buch** plural, we make a vowel change (indicated by an **Umlaut**) and we add *-er* to the end of the word.

Buch ⟶ Bücher

The pronunciation of **Bücher** is different from the pronunciation of its singular form **Buch** in the following ways:

- The *bu* at the beginning of **Bücher** has sort of a *you* sound, like the beginning of the word *beauty*.
- The sound of the *u*, with its **Umlaut**, sounds like the *oo* in boot, but with your lips rounded. It sounds similar to the *ew* in the English word *few*.
- Because of the vowel change of the letter *u*, the sound of the *ch* part of the word changes from a scraping sound to more of a whooshing sound, like the sound of the letter *h* that begins the word *huge*.

So with all this in mind, the word **Bücher** sounds something like *BYEW-shah*.

Zeitung is feminine. In German, the letter *z* sounds like *ts*. Therefore **Zeitung** sounds something like *TSY-toong*. To make **Zeitung** plural, add *-en* like this:

Zeitung ⟶ Zeitungen

EXERCISES

1. **Der Hund hat die Zeitung!**
2. **Meine Schwester hat ihre Bücher und mein Vater hat seine Zeitung.**
3. **Wir haben die Bücher.**
4. **Frau Jones hat Geld, aber Herr Smith hat kein Geld.**
5. **Mein Bruder hat einen Hund.**
6. **Ihr Vater hat zwei Töchter, aber er hat keine Söhne.**
7. **Ihre Mutter hat sieben Katzen.**

8. **Ihr Bruder hat einen Hund, aber er hat keine Katze.**
9. **Ihr seid meine Schwestern, aber sie sind meine Brüder.**
10. **Meine Freundin hat ein Auto. Ich habe auch ein Auto.**

Answers on page 197.

LESSON 84

NEW WORD   **unser**

MEANING   *our*

Our new word for this lesson is another **ein** word. It is similar to the word **ihr** because it really is an **ein** word even though it doesn't look like one.

	MASCULINE	FEMININE	NEUTER	PLURAL
NOMINATIVE (SUBJ./PRED. NOM.)	unser	unsere	unser	unsere
ACCUSATIVE (DIRECT OBJECT)	unseren	unsere	unser	unsere

EXERCISES

1. **Sie haben unseren Hund!**
2. **Er hat unsere Zeitung.**
3. **Unser Vater ist sein Bruder.**
4. **Der Hund hat unser Buch!**
5. **Wir haben unsere Bücher und meine Mutter hat ihre Zeitung.**
6. **Ihr habt unsere Zeitung.**
7. **Deine Freundinnen haben unser Auto.**
8. **Sie haben acht Dollar, aber wir haben kein Geld.**
9. **Herr Smith hat drei Hunde und eine Katze.**
10. **Ich bin eine Katze, aber du bist ein Hund.**

Answers on page 197.

LESSON 85

NEW WORD   **euer**

MEANING   *y'all's*

PRONUNCIATION TIP: This sounds something like *OY-ah*.

Euer, our new word for this lesson, is yet another **ein** word. It's a possessive adjective that means *your*, but for when you are speaking to more than one person. Therefore the way we will tranlsate this word in the answer key is with the word…um…*y'all's*.

Now, you might be thinking to yourself, "Hey, that's stupid. *Y'all's* isn't even a real word!" And you may be right—it could be stupid. But before you send this book flying across the room and into the trash can, consider these points:

- The reason we are doing this is to help you differentiate the second person singular (**dein**) from the second person plural (**euer**). If we translated both of them as *your*, it would be more confusing for you since the word *your* in English can be either singular or plural.
- The purpose of the book is to teach you German, not English.
- And lastly, remember that as you learn you should have fun and not take everything too seriously.

As you study the various forms of **euer**, you may notice that some forms of **euer** are missing the letter *e*. For example, in the nominative feminine form, you might expect to see **euere**, which is **euer** with an *e* added. And that is a legitimate form of the word—but it is more common to see the spelling without the *e*, which is **eure**.

	MASCULINE	FEMININE	NEUTER	PLURAL
NOMINATIVE (SUBJ./PRED. NOM.)	euer	eure	euer	eure
ACCUSATIVE (DIRECT OBJECT)	euren	eure	euer	eure

95

1. **Ich habe euren Stuhl.**
2. **Eure Schwester ist meine Freundin.**
3. **Wir haben euer Auto.**
4. **Euer Hund hat unsere Zeitung.**
5. **Er hat eure Bücher.**
6. **Das Mädchen hat seine Bücher.**
7. **Meine Schwester hat eure Bücher.**
8. **Wir haben ihr Geld.**
9. **Frau Smith hat fünf Hunde und zwei Katzen.**
10. **Wir sind Schwestern und er ist unser Bruder.**

Answers on page 197.

LESSON 86

"IHR" CAN ALSO MEAN "THEIR"

We really, truly aren't trying to confuse you…but we are now presenting the word **ihr** to you for the third time. As we learned recently, the word **ihr** can be the possessive adjective *her* (as in *her book*), and as a pronoun it can be the pronoun *y'all* (as in *y'all are late*). But as you can see from the title of this lesson, **ihr** can also be the possessive adjective *their*.

Like the **ihr** that means *her*, this **ihr** is also an **ein** word. Observe the various forms of this word in the chart below.

	MASCULINE	FEMININE	NEUTER	PLURAL
NOMINATIVE (SUBJ./PRED. NOM.)	ihr	ihre	ihr	ihre
ACCUSATIVE (DIRECT OBJECT)	ihren	ihre	ihr	ihre

Since the word **ihr** can mean more than one thing, you'll have to use context to understand whether **ihr** means *her* or *their*. Observe this example:

> **Die Frau ist meine Schwester und ich habe ihr Buch.** *(The woman is my sister and I have her book.)*

In this example, the first part of the sentence talks about someone's sister. Therefore, when you get to the second part of the sentence, you know that the word *book* is referring back to the female from the first part. She is the book's owner. This context helps you to know that the word **ihr** in the second sentence means *her*. But what about a sentence like this?

> **Ich habe ihr Buch.**

In this example, there isn't enough information for us to know the corresponding adjective of the person or persons who own the book. Therefore, if you were going to translate this sentence into English, you would not know whether to translate **ihr** as *her* or *their*. If we have an exercise like that in this book, in the answer key we will put *her/their* so you will know that **ihr** can be translated as either one.

Keeping these grammar rules straight might seem confusing right now, but the key here is practice and repetition. Keep practicing, and these forms will soon become second nature.

EXERCISES

1. **Sie haben ihren Tisch.**
2. **Er hat ihre Bücher.**
3. **Wir haben ihr Auto.**
4. **Der Hund hat ihre Zeitung!**
5. **Wir haben ihre Bücher.**
6. **Eure Schwester ist meine Freundin.**
7. **Sie haben euren Hund.**
8. **Sie hat ihre Zeitung und ich habe unsere Bücher.**
9. **Der Junge hat sein Buch.**
10. **Sie sind meine Eltern. Sie haben kein Geld.**

Answers on page 197.

LESSON 87

REVIEW OF POSSESSIVE ADJECTIVES

In the preceding pages we purposely provided a prodigiously potent pile of possessive adjectives. You now know how to say words like *my, your, his, her, its, our,* (GULP) *y'all's,* and *their* in German.

When it comes to verbs, we have talked a lot about person and number—and in doing so, you have learned the difference between first person, second person and third person. But you can also think of possessive adjectives like that. **Mein**, for example, refers to the speaker, so it is first person singular. **Dein** refers to the person being spoken to (just one), so it is second person singular, and so on and so forth. So if we put all the possessive adjectives you know into a chart, it would look like this:

	SINGULAR	PLURAL
FIRST PERSON	**mein**	**unser**
SECOND PERSON	**dein**	**euer**
THIRD PERSON	**sein/ihr/sein**	**ihr**

Use this chart to review the possessive adjectives that you have learned so far. And, for extra practice, try to use them to make up sentences verbally on the spot. The more practice you get speaking and using these adjectives, the easier it will be to read them.

LESSON 88

NEW WORD **Hunger / Durst**

MEANING *hunger / thirst*

This is how you say *I am hungry* in German:

Ich habe Hunger.

Ich habe, as you already know, means *I have*. And the masculine word **Hunger** means *hunger*. So literally, **ich habe Hunger** means *I have hunger*.

If you want to say *I am thirsty*, the wording is the same:

Ich habe Durst.

The masculine word **Durst** means *thirst*. So literally, **ich habe Durst** means *I have thirst*. But we translate it into English as *I am thirsty*.

If someone else is hungry or thirsty, just use the different forms of **ich habe** along with **Hunger** or **Durst**, as shown in these examples:

- **Sie hat Hunger.** (*She is hungry.*)
- **Wir haben Durst.** (*We are thirsty.*)

To say someone is not hungry or thirsty, use **kein** to say that someone does not have hunger or thirst. Since the nouns **Hunger** and **Durst** in this context are masculine direct objects, you'll need to use the form **keinen** with them, like this:

- **Sie hat keinen Hunger.** (*She is not hungry.*)
- **Wir haben keinen Durst.** (*We are not thirsty.*)

The following exercises will give you some practice using these expressions.

EXERCISES

1. **Ihr habt Hunger.**
2. **Er hat keinen Hunger.**
3. **Seine Katze hat Durst.**
4. **Unsere Hunde haben Durst.**

99

5. **Du hast ihr Auto nicht.**
6. **Ihre Tochter hat ein Auto, aber mein Sohn hat kein Auto.**
7. **Mein Hund hat Hunger, aber meine Katze hat keinen Hunger.**
8. **Wir haben eure Bücher und auch eure Zeitungen.**
9. **Sie hat ihr Geld—zwei Dollar und sieben Euro.**
10. **Die Kinder sind unsere Söhne und Töchter.**

Answers on page 197.

LESSON 89

NEW WORD   **Essen / Futter**

MEANING   *food* (for humans) / *food* (for pets)

PRONUNCIATION TIP: **Essen** rhymes with *lesson*.

Essen and **Futter** both mean *food*, but with one important difference: **Essen** is human food and **Futter** is pet food. So you'll give **Essen** to your kids, but you'll give **Futter** to Fido and Fluffy.

Essen and **Futter** are neuter, so they need a neuter article such as **das** or **kein**.

EXERCISES

1. **Der Hund hat unser Essen.**
2. **Wir haben kein Essen, aber meine Freunde haben Essen.**
3. **Die Katzen haben ihr Futter.**
4. **Meine Kinder haben Hunger, aber ich habe kein Essen.**
5. **Euer Hund hat Futter.**
6. **Dein Sohn hat Hunger, aber er hat kein Geld.**
7. **Eure Söhne haben ihre Bücher.**
8. **Meine Mutter hat ihr Geld—neun Dollar und fünf Euro.**
9. **Eure Katzen haben Durst.**
10. **Du bist mein Freund und er ist mein Bruder.**

Answers on page 198.

LESSON 90

NEW WORD **Wasser**

MEANING *water*

Wasser is a neuter noun, so it needs a neuter article like **das** or **kein**.

EXERCISES

1. **Ich habe Durst, aber ich habe kein Wasser.**
2. **Meine Katze hat Durst, aber sie hat kein Wasser.**
3. **Eure Katzen haben Futter, aber sie haben kein Wasser.**
4. **Der Junge hat Durst, aber er hat kein Wasser.**
5. **Meine Katze hat Hunger, aber sie hat kein Futter.**
6. **Mein Bruder hat kein Geld. Seine Frau hat auch kein Geld.**
7. **Unsere Kinder haben Hunger und Durst.**
8. **Eure Tochter hat euren Hund.**
9. **Sie ist meine Mutter und ihre Schwester ist Frau Jones.**
10. **Mein Vater hat seine Zeitung.**

Answers on page 198.

LESSON 91

NEW WORD   **ich brauche**

MEANING   *I need*

When we learned about **ich habe**, we learned each form one at a time. But now that you have some experience working with verbs, there is no need to learn every new verb one form at a time. So, in this lesson, we are going to give you all the forms of **ich brauche** at the same time.

	SINGULAR	PLURAL
FIRST PERSON	**ich brauche**	**wir brauchen**
SECOND PERSON	**du brauchst**	**ihr braucht**
THIRD PERSON	**er/sie/es braucht**	**sie brauchen**

EXERCISES

1. **Unser Hund braucht Futter.**
2. **Ich brauche eine Zeitung und Essen.**
3. **Wir haben Durst. Wir brauchen Wasser.**
4. **Seine Kinder brauchen Essen, aber sie haben kein Geld.**
5. **Sie brauchen eine Katze.**
6. **Der Hund hat Hunger. Er braucht Futter.**
7. **Du bist keine Katze. Du bist ein Hund.**
8. **Eure Kinder brauchen Bücher.**
9. **Ihre Mutter braucht einen Hund.**
10. **Mein Freund hat ein Auto, aber er braucht sein Auto nicht.**

Answers on page 198.

102

LESSON 92

INDIRECT OBJECTS

You already know that a direct object is a noun that is the target of the action being performed by the subject of the sentence. But in grammar, there is also something called the *indirect object*. An indirect object is the party that is receiving or benefiting from the action being performed by the subject. In English, indirect objects are often indicated by words like *to* or *for*. In each of the following examples, the indirect object is underlined:

- He gave the book to <u>Johnny</u>.
- She told a story to the <u>class</u>.
- She bought some gifts for her <u>friends</u>.
- He showed his rock collection to <u>Mr. Green.</u>

In each of these sentences, the subject of the sentence gave the direct object to the indirect object. Again, notice that the indirect object is that party that is receiving or benefiting.

In everyday English, we often say the same kind of statement but with a different word order, putting the indirect object before the direct object. Let's observe those same sentences shown above, but this time with this alternate wording.

- He gave <u>Johnny</u> the book.
- She told the <u>class</u> a story.
- She bought her <u>friends</u> some gifts.
- He showed <u>Mr. Green</u> his rock collection.

By the way, take care not to confuse indirect objects with objects of the preposition. Consider the following example:

I sailed to the island.

In this example, the word *to* is just a preposition, not indicating an indirect object.

In the following exercises, see if you can identify both the direct object and the indirect object.

EXERCISES

1. I loaned the money to my friend.
2. We donated money to the charity.
3. He showed the class an example.
4. Let's get some curtains for the house.
5. Henry got some seeds for the garden.
6. They made us some sandwiches.
7. He told the judge his story.
8. The band played another song for the audience.
9. I brought copies for everyone.
10. My mother bought me a shirt.

Answers on page 198.

LESSON 93

THE DATIVE CASE

In our study of the German language we have learned about cases and how they function in a sentence. For example, the subject of the sentence is in the nominative case while the direct object is in the accusative case.

In the last lesson, we learned that the indirect object is the party in the sentence that is receiving or benefiting. In German there is a special case dedicated to the indirect object. That case is called the *dative* case (pronounced *DAY-tiv*).

In German, the way we indicate the dative case is by changing the definite article and the various **ein** words. Here is a chart showing the dative forms of **der**, the definite article.

	MASCULINE	FEMININE	NEUTER	PLURAL
NOMINATIVE (SUBJ./PRED. NOM.)	der	die	das	die
ACCUSATIVE (DIRECT OBJECT)	den	die	das	die
DATIVE (INDIRECT OBJECT)	dem	der	dem	den

Sooooo…we aren't trying to confuse you here, but, as you may have noticed, there are a couple of dative forms that look like forms from other cases. For example, the femimine form of the dative is **der**, which is the same as the masculine nominative form (these two forms are connected with a dotted line so you can see the connection). Also, the dative plural form, **den**, is the same as the masculine accusative singular form (these two forms are also connected with a dotted line).

Here's how this affects you: when you are reading German and you see the word **der**, you'll need to figure out if it's a nominative masculine or dative feminine. In order to do this, you'll need to observe the context and the gender of the noun it goes with.

Likewise, when you see the word **den**, you'll need to figure out if it's a masculine accusative article or a dative plural article. Again, observe the context and think about the gender of the noun it goes with.

The word **dem** isn't so hard—it can only be dative. The only question is whether it's masculine or neuter, and that will be obvious judging from the gender of the noun it accompanies.

The dative forms of **ein** words aren't as ambiguous or confusing. In the chart below, observe the various forms of **mein**.

	MASCULINE	FEMININE	NEUTER	PLURAL
NOMINATIVE (SUBJ./PRED. NOM.)	**mein**	**meine**	**mein**	**meine**
ACCUSATIVE (DIRECT OBJECT)	**meinen**	**meine**	**mein**	**meine**
DATIVE (INDIRECT OBJECT)	**meinem**	**meiner**	**meinem**	**meinen**

Notice that the only duplicate is the dative plural, which looks the same as the accusative singular. Like **dem**, **meinem** can only be dative—either masculine or neuter. Also, **meiner** doesn't look like anything else, so it can only be dative feminine.

For now, study these forms, and in the next lesson we will begin to use them in sentences.

LESSON 94

USING THE DATIVE CASE

Now that we have studied the indirect objects and the dative forms of **der** and **ein**, we are ready to begin using the dative case in German sentences. Let's start with a simple English sentence, and then translate it into German.

Let's make up a sentence about giving a book to a man. We could word this sample sentence two different ways:

- I am giving the book to the man.
- I am giving the man the book.

In the first sentence we know that the word *man* is the indirect object because the word *to* tells us that the book is going to the man. But in the second sentence, we don't have the word *to*. Instead, the way the sentence is worded tells us that the man is the one receiving the book. When we say *I give the man the book*, we put the indirect object first, then the direct object, and that certain word order tells us what is going on. Here's the important part: in a German sentence, the word order will be like the second sentence, with the indirect object first, before the direct object. So, if that sentence were in German, it would be worded like this:

I am giving the man the book.

In that sentence, the man is the indirect object—so if this were a German sentence, we would need to put the word for *man* in the dative case. We do that by changing its definite article to **dem**. Therefore if this were a German sentence, the part about *the man* would be **dem Mann**. Let's put that into our sentence:

I am giving **dem Mann** the book.

So with the dative article **dem**, we can see that the word **Mann** is the indirect object. Notice that the dative case indicates the indirect object without the help of a word such as *to* or *for*. The idea of *to* or *for* is embedded into the dative case itself.

Now, let's translate the direct object into German, too. Since **Buch** is neuter, the accusative form of the definite article will be **das**. So let's add **das Buch** to our sentence:

I am giving **dem Mann das Buch**.

In the next lesson, you'll learn how to say *give* in German—and then you'll be able to say this entire sentence in German.

LESSON 95

NEW WORD   **ich gebe**

MEANING   *I give*

Observe the various forms of **ich gebe** in this handy chart:

	SINGULAR	PLURAL
FIRST PERSON	**ich gebe**	**wir geben**
SECOND PERSON	**du gibst**	**ihr gebt**
THIRD PERSON	**er/sie/es gibt**	**sie geben**

Now that you know this new verb, we can make even more complex German sentences—sentences with both a direct object and an indirect object. Here's the example sentence we were working with in the last lesson, but with our new verb for this lesson:

Ich gebe dem Mann das Buch. *(I am giving the man the book.)*

Later, you'll learn about situations in which the indirect object can go after the direct object. But for now, remember that the indirect object needs to go before the direct object.

Quick review: the indirect object will have a dative definite article such as **dem**, **der**, **dem**, or **den**. Any dative **ein** word will have forms such as **meinem**, **meiner**, **meinem**, and **meiner**.

1. **Wir geben dem Kind das Geld.**
2. **Ich gebe dem Mann ein Auto.**
3. **Er gibt seiner Tochter das Auto.**
4. **Sie geben deinem Kind die Bücher.**
5. **Sie gibt ihrem Mann das Geld.**
6. **Du gibst eurer Tochter die Zeitung.**
7. **Helga gibt ihrem Kind das Geld.**
8. **Ihr gebt dem Hund Futter und Wasser.**
9. **Unsere Katze hat Durst und sie braucht Wasser.**
10. **Ihr seid Schwestern und wir sind Brüder.**

Answers on page 198.

LESSON 96

NOUNS CAN CHANGE, TOO

By this point in the book, you have some good experience working with noun cases. You now know the form and function of the nominative case, the accusative case, and most recently, the dative case. Finally, at the end of this book, you will learn about the one remaining case.

When you look at a noun, how do you know what case it is? For example, can you tell what case this noun is?

Mann

By itself, you can't tell what case the word **Mann** is. Just by its appearance, it could be nominative, accusative, or dative. By itself, the noun **Mann** looks the same no matter what case it is. But what about this?

den Mann

Now that **Mann** has an article with it, you can tell that it is in the accusative case. Since the noun itself does not change, we depend on the article to indicate what the case of the noun is.

But here's the new thing we need to tell you: sometimes, instead of just the article changing, the noun itself changes. *For some nouns, we will need to add the letter* n *to the end of the dative plural form.*

Here's the way it works: if a noun ends with the letter *n* or *s* in the nominative plural form, the dative plural stays the same as the nominative plural form. But if the nominative plural form does not end with the letter *n* or *s*, we must add the letter *n* to the end of the dative plural form.

Let's look at a few examples. For the noun **Frau**, the nominative plural form is **Frauen**. It ends with the letter *n*, so the dative plural form is the same as the nominative plural form.

	SINGULAR	PLURAL
NOMINATIVE (SUBJ./PRED. NOM.)	Frau	Frauen
ACCUSATIVE (DIRECT OBJECT)	Frau	Frauen
DATIVE (INDIRECT OBJECT)	Frau	Frauen

SAME!

Now let's look at another noun, **Mann**. For the noun **Mann**, the nominative plural form is **Männer**. It does not end with the letter *n*, so in the dative plural we must add the letter *n*, like this:

	SINGULAR	PLURAL
NOMINATIVE (SUBJ./PRED. NOM.)	Mann	Männer
ACCUSATIVE (DIRECT OBJECT)	Mann	Männer
DATIVE (INDIRECT OBJECT)	Mann	Männern

NOT SAME!

Now let's look at the neuter loan word **Auto**. If the nominative plural ends in *-s*, like **Autos**, we do not need to add an *-n* in the dative plural.

	SINGULAR	PLURAL	
NOMINATIVE (SUBJ./PRED. NOM.)	**Auto**	**Autos**	
ACCUSATIVE (DIRECT OBJECT)	**Auto**	**Autos**	SAME!
DATIVE (INDIRECT OBJECT)	**Auto**	**Autos**	

So as you can see from this lesson, not only the articles and **ein** words change spelling for the different cases—the noun itself can change too. Remember this important concept because in the future you'll see it even more as we study one final noun case.

Here's a quick review of the rules: if the nominative plural form ends with the letter *n*, the dative plural form doesn't change—it's the same as the nominative plural. But if the nominative plural does not end with the letter *n*, we have to add the letter *n* to the dative plural form. For any noun that has a nominative plural ending in *-s*, the dative plural stays the same as the nominative plural.

In the exercises below, find the dative plural form of each noun. Work from the nominative singular to the nominative plural to the dative plural, like this:

Mutter ⟶ Mütter ⟶ Müttern

You'll get the hang of it after you practice it a few times.

EXERCISES

1. **Mädchen**
2. **Junge**
3. **Bruder**
4. **Schwester**
5. **Freund**
6. **Freundin**
7. **Sohn**
8. **Tochter**
9. **Kind**
10. **Vater**

Answers on page 198.

LESSON 97

NEW WORD   **Geschenk**

MEANING   *gift*

The word **Geschenk** is neuter. To make it plural, add an *e* to the end, like this:

Geschenk ⟶ Geschenke

Before you do the exercises, remember that for most nouns, the dative plural will have the letter *n* at the end. For example, for the word **Mann** the dative plural would look like this:

Mann ⟶ Männer ⟶ Männern

So in German, *to the men* or *for the men* would be **den Männern**.

EXERCISES

1. **Ich gebe dem Mann das Geschenk.**
2. **Ich gebe den Männern die Geschenke.**
3. **Wir geben meinen Schwestern ein Geschenk.**
4. **Ihr braucht ein Geschenk.**
5. **Meine Schwestern geben unseren Eltern das Auto.**
6. **Du brauchst Essen, aber du hast kein Geld.**
7. **Wir geben den Kindern unser Geschenk.**
8. **Ihr Hund braucht Wasser. Sein Hund braucht auch Wasser.**
9. **Meine Freundin gibt ihrer Schwester ihren Hund.**
10. **Das Mädchen gibt dem Hund sein Futter.**

Answers on page 199.

LESSON 98

NEW WORD   **ich kaufe**

MEANING   *I buy*

Take some time to memorize these forms along with their accompanying pronouns.

	SINGULAR	PLURAL
FIRST PERSON	**ich kaufe**	**wir kaufen**
SECOND PERSON	**du kaufst**	**ihr kauft**
THIRD PERSON	**er/sie/es kauft**	**sie kaufen**

If you are buying something for someone, you should put the recipient in the dative case. In this example, the recipient has a definite article.

Ich kaufe dem Vater ein Geschenk. *(I am buying the father a gift.)*

And this one has an **ein** word:

Ich kaufe meinem Vater ein Geschenk. *(I am buying my father a gift.)*

Remember that the indirect object needs to come first, so we put **dem Vater** and **meinem Vater** before **Geschenk**, which is the direct object.

EXERCISES

1. **Ich kaufe meiner Mutter ein Geschenk.**
2. **Meine Schwestern kaufen unseren Eltern ein Geschenk.**
3. **Ihr kauft den Katzen Futter.**
4. **Sie kauft ihrem Sohn ein Auto.**

5. **Ihr kauft euren Eltern einen Tisch.**
6. **Wir kaufen seinen Kindern ein Geschenk.**
7. **Die Jungen brauchen Wasser.**
8. **Die Hunde haben Hunger und sie brauchen Futter.**
9. **Du gibst meinem Bruder deine Zeitung.**
10. **Ihr seid unsere Freundinnen.**

Answers on page 199.

LESSON 99

STEMS AND PERSONAL ENDINGS

You may have noticed by now that there is a pattern to the endings of German verbs. For instance, first person singular verbs typically end in *-e*, as seen in verb forms like **habe**, **brauche**, **gebe**, and **kaufe**.

In the last lesson, you learned the new verb **ich kaufe**. In this lesson, let's take a closer look at the various forms of that verb. For convenience, here are all the forms of **ich kaufe** again:

	SINGULAR	PLURAL
FIRST PERSON	**ich kaufe**	**wir kaufen**
SECOND PERSON	**du kaufst**	**ihr kauft**
THIRD PERSON	**er/sie/es kauft**	**sie kaufen**

Notice that each form of this verb starts with **kauf-**. That part of the verb is called the *stem*. After the stem, each different form of the verb has its own special, individual ending. If we isolated those endings and put them into a chart, the chart would look like this:

	SINGULAR	PLURAL
FIRST PERSON	**-e**	**-en**
SECOND PERSON	**-st**	**-t**
THIRD PERSON	**-t**	**-en**

We will call these endings *personal endings*. They show whether a verb is first person, second person, or third person, and also whether the verb is singular or plural.

In German, there are regular verbs and irregular verbs. **Ich kaufe** is a regular verb. This means that any regular verb you come across will follow the pattern of endings you see in the chart above. You can take the stem of the verb and add the endings, creating each verb form in a predictable way. In short, a regular verb follows the expected pattern. You can make the forms of a regular verb with this formula:

stem + personal ending = verb form

Then there are irregular verbs—that is, verbs that do not follow the expected pattern. For these verbs, you can't use any kind of formula to make the different verb forms. Instead, you just have to memorize them.

Take, for example, **ich habe**, which is an irregular verb. The stem of **ich habe** is **hab-**. Therefore if **ich habe** were a regular verb, we could make the second person singular form by taking the stem, **hab-**, and adding the second person singular ending to it, which is **-st**. That would give us **habst**. But since **ich habe** is irregular, that formula doesn't work. The second person singular form isn't **habst**, it's **hast**.

Unfortunately, you have only learned two regular verbs so far in this book: **ich kaufe** and **ich brauche**. All the other verbs you know are irregular. But even though you only know a couple of regular verbs, we still wanted to explain stems and personal endings to you just for your own knowledge.

LESSON 100

STEM-CHANGING VERBS

In the last lesson, we learned about verb stems and personal endings. That's an important concept that will take you a long way in German—and you'll find that same thing happening with verbs in other languages such as Latin, Spanish, and French.

In this lesson, we want to tell you one additional thing about German verb stems. In German, some verbs have a special change that takes place in the stem of the second person singular and third person singular forms. Take a look at the different forms of the verb **ich gebe** in the chart below, and see if you notice anything about the second person singular form and third person singular form (these forms are circled in the chart).

	SINGULAR	PLURAL
FIRST PERSON	**ich gebe**	**wir geben**
SECOND PERSON	**du gibst**	**ihr gebt**
THIRD PERSON	**er/sie/es gibt**	**sie geben**

Ich gebe is what we call a *stem-changing verb*. That's because...um...the stem changes. You see, the real stem of this verb is **geb-**. That's the stem that you find in the first person singular, first person plural, second person plural, and third person plural. But in the second person singular and third person singular, the stem is **gib-**. The stem changes for those two particular forms, and so that's why we call it a stem-changing verb.

If you know which German verbs are stem-changing verbs, it will make it easier for you to remember the different forms. For the remainder of the book, if we see any more stem-changing verbs, we will point them out to you.

115

LESSON 101

THE PRESENT TENSE

In this book, all the verbs that we will learn about are present tense verbs. This means that the action happening is in the here and now. But did you know that there is more than one kind of present tense?

In English, you might see a sentence like this:

> I give gifts.

Even though you may not be giving someone a gift right now, it is still a general statement that happens sometimes, so we use the present tense to express it. This kind of present tense is called the *simple present*.

Contrast that with this similar English sentence:

> I am giving gifts.

In this sentence, the verb *giving* communicates a different shade of meaning than in the first example. Here, you are saying that you currently give gifts. It suggests that the action is current and ongoing with more of a sense of currency than if you said *I give gifts*. This kind of present tense is called the *present progressive*. It's progressive because the action is ongoing at this very moment.

So how does this relate to German verbs? What we want you to understand is that in English, there is both a simple present and a present progressive, but in German there is not. In German, there is only one way to say something in the present tense. Observe this German sentence:

Ich gebe Geschenke.

If you translate this sentence into English, you could translate it as either *I give gifts* or *I am giving gifts*. How will you know whether to translate a verb using simple present or present progressive? Look at the context, and that should make it clear. For example, if you see a German sentence that contains the verb **Ich gebe** and you aren't sure what the best translation is, try translating it as both *I give* and *I am giving* and see which one sounds better. Don't worry if we choose one translation for the answer key and you chose another—often either one works just fine.

LESSON 102

NEW WORD   **Handy**

MEANING   *mobile phone*

Handy is neuter, so it needs a neuter article such as **das** or **ein**. The plural form is **Handys**.

Mobile phones, cell phones, smart phones: as they become the usual way people communicate, people are starting to call them *phones* instead of cell phones or mobile phones. So in this book, we will translate the word **Handy** into English simply as *phone*.

EXERCISES

1. **Ich gebe meinem Bruder das Handy.**
2. **Deine Schwester hat mein Handy.**
3. **Mein Bruder gibt seinem Freund sein Handy.**
4. **Meine Mutter hat dein Handy.**
5. **Ich kaufe meinen Töchtern ein Handy.**
6. **Wir haben kein Handy, kein Auto und kein Geld.**
7. **Mein Freund hat zwei Handys. Ich habe auch zwei Handys.**
8. **Wir geben den Kindern Geschenke.**
9. **Die Kinder haben Hunger, aber sie haben kein Essen.**
10. **Wir kaufen meinen Söhnen Handys.**

Answers on page 199.

LESSON 103

MORE ABOUT THE DATIVE CASE

Now that you have some experience working with the dative case, it's time to broaden your view of the dative case and how it is used.

In German, so far you have seen verbs working with the accusative case—but some verbs, because of their meaning, interact more naturally with the dative case. Consider the following sentence:

I help my father.

If you were to analyze the grammar of that sentence, you would conclude that the word *father* is the direct object. But what if we reword the sentence a little, like this:

I am giving help to my father.

Now, with this wording, the word *father* goes from being the direct object to being the indirect object (with the word *help* as the direct object). After all, the father is the party in the sentence that is receiving or benefiting—in this case, receiving the help, or benefiting from the help. Let's try yet another wording for this sentence:

I am being helpful toward my father.

In this wording, the grammar works differently. The word I is the subject, and the verb is a verb of being or existing, not an action verb. And, as you already know, a verb of being or existing cannot generate a direct object. So again, the word father here is not a direct object.

So, the point here is that there are some verbs that in English would take a direct object, whereas that same verb in German will naturally work with the dative case.

LESSON 104

NEW WORD **ich helfe**

MEANING *I help*

In the last lesson you learned that some German verbs work with the dative case instead of the accusative case. Our new verb for this lesson is one of those verbs.

In addition to being a verb which takes the dative case, **ich helfe** is also a stem-changing verb. The "real" stem for this verb is **help-**, which you can see is the stem in the first person singular, first person plural, second person plural, and third person plural. But the second person singular and third person singular deviate from this stem and instead have the stem **hilf-**. These two forms are circled in the chart below.

	SINGULAR	PLURAL
FIRST PERSON	**ich helfe**	**wir helfen**
SECOND PERSON	**du hilfst**	**ihr helft**
THIRD PERSON	**er/sie/es hilft**	**sie helfen**

Remember again that the dative case indicates the indirect object in a sentence—that is, the party that is receiving or benefiting in the sentence. Our new verb for this lesson takes the dative case, like this:

Ich helfe meinem Vater. *(I help my father.)*

Again, notice that **meinem** is dative, not accusative. Think of the sentence as meaning *I am giving help to my father* or *I am being helpful toward my father*. That will help you to picture in your mind this verb taking the dative case instead of the accusative.

119

If you want to say that someone is *not* helping someone, put the word **nicht** after the indirect object, like this:

Ich helfe meinem Vater nicht. *(I do not help my father.)*

In the exercises below, get some practice with using **ich helfe** with the dative case.

EXERCISES

1. **Ich helfe meinem Vater.**
2. **Ich helfe den Kindern.**
3. **Du hilfst ihrer Mutter.**
4. **Wir helfen deinem Vater.**
5. **Sie helfen den Hunden.**
6. **Ich helfe deinem Vater nicht.**
7. **Wir kaufen unseren Söhnen Autos.**
8. **Ich habe kein Handy, aber mein Mann hat ein Handy.**
9. **Das Mädchen hat sein Buch, aber meine Söhne haben kein Buch.**
10. **Ihr gebt meinen Schwestern Geld.**

Answers on page 199.

LESSON 105

ADVERBS

An adverb is a word that describes a verb. An adverb can tell us *when* an action is happening, *how* it is happening, or *where* it is happening. In the examples below, the adverb in each sentence is underlined.

- We went to the park <u>yesterday</u>.
- I drive <u>cautiously</u>.
- I live <u>nearby</u>.

The word "yesterday" describes when the action of going to the park happened. The word "cautiously" describes how the action of driving happens, and the word "nearby" describes where the action of living happens.

But you aren't limited to just one-word adverbs if you want to describe the action taking place. A phrase made up of several words can have an adverbial meaning or quality to it, describing how the action is happening. These phrases are called *adverbial phrases.* In each of the examples below, notice that the underlined words make up an adverbial phrase which describes the action.

- We went to the park <u>after lunch</u>.
- I drive <u>with great caution</u>.
- I live <u>across the river</u>.

In the first example, the phrase "after lunch" was adverbial in the sense that it tells us when the action of going to the park happened. In the second example, the phrase "with great caution" was adverbial in the sense that it told us how the action of the driving is happening. And in the last example, the phrase "across the river" is a prepositional phrase that is adverbial because it tells us where the action of living is happening.

In the next lesson, you will learn your first adverbial phrase in German. As you learn about them, you will need to pay special attention to word order—that is, the place in the sentence where the adverbial phrase must go. We will start with very simple sentences, but as we go along we will gradually show you more about the expected word order associated with adverbs and adverbial phrases in different kinds of sentences.

LESSON 106

NEW WORD   **jeden Tag**

MEANING   *every day*

The word **jeden** is an adjective. As you already know from studying possessive adjectives, adjectives can have different forms for different cases and genders. In the expression **jeden Tag**, **jeden** is masculine because it needs to agree with the masculine noun **Tag**. Furthermore, in German, this kind of statement uses the accusative case (it's a long story).

You can use the adjective **jeden** with other words, too. **Morgen** means *morning*, so **jeden Morgen** means *every morning*. **Abend** means *evening*, so **jeden Abend** means *every evening*. The word **Woche** means week—but it's feminine, so the form of **jeden** changes to **jede** and you get **jede Woche**, which means *every week*.

As we mentioned in the last lesson, you must pay attention to word order when working with adverbs and adverbial phrases. Let's look at some examples to see where an adverb or adverbial phrase would go in a German sentence.

Here's a sentence with just a subject, verb, and adverbial phrase. It's not a very good sentence, but we are just putting it here as an example for demonstrating word order. In a sentence like this, you will typically put the adverbial phrase after the verb:

Ich helfe jeden Tag. *(I help every day.)*

Here's another kind of sentence, this time with a subject, verb, direct object, and adverbial phrase. In this kind of sentence, an adverb or adverbial phrase will usually go after the verb but before the direct object, like this:

Ich kaufe jede Woche Essen. *(I buy food every week.)*

If the sentence has an indirect object but no direct object (as often seen in sentences with **helfen**), the adverb or adverbial phrase will generally come after the verb, like this:

Ich helfe meinem Vater jeden Tag. *(I help my father every day.)*

122

If the sentence has both a direct object and an indirect object (pay attention to this) the adverb or adverbial phrase will typically come after the indirect object but before the direct object, like this:

Ich kaufe meiner Tochter <u>jede Woche</u> ein Geschenk. *(I buy my daughter a gift <u>every week</u>.)*

There is much, much more to learn about German word order, but for now, these examples will suffice to help you understand and speak the exercises that we have in this part of the book.

EXERCISES

1. **Ich helfe seinem Vater jeden Tag.**
2. **Ich gebe meinen Katzen jeden Morgen Futter.**
3. **Ihr kauft euren Hunden jede Woche Futter.**
4. **Er hilft seiner Mutter jede Woche.**
5. **Du gibst den Kindern jeden Abend Geschenke.**
6. **Ich gebe meiner Frau jeden Tag mein Handy.**
7. **Sie helfen den Kindern nicht.**
8. **Ihre Hunde brauchen jeden Tag Futter.**
9. **Wir brauchen Essen, aber mein Mann hat kein Geld.**
10. **Seine Freunde haben Hunger, aber wir haben kein Essen.**

Answers on page 199.

LESSON 107

NEW WORD   **mir / dir**

MEANING   *me / you* (dative case forms)

So far, the only pronouns you have learned are the kind that can be either the subject of a sentence or a predicate nominative. These are pronouns like **ich**, **du**, **er**, **sie**, **es**, **wir**, **ihr**, and **sie**. These pronouns, although you may not have realized it yet, are nominative case pronouns. But like the definite article, **ein** words, and nouns, pronouns can be in different cases, too.

So if you think of the pronoun **ich** as being nominative, then the dative form of that pronoun would be **mir**, one of our new words for this lesson. Observe the chart below.

NOMINATIVE (SUBJ./PRED. NOM.)	**ich**
ACCUSATIVE (DIRECT OBJECT)	
DATIVE (INDIRECT OBJECT)	mir

Mir is the dative way to say *me*, so as an indirect object it can mean *to me* or *for me*. Or it can be used with verbs that take the dative case, such as **ich helfe**.

Here are a couple of examples of how you could use **mir** in a sentence:

- **Meine Mutter kauft mir ein Auto.** *(My mother is buying me a car.)*
- **Mein Bruder hilft mir nicht.** *(My brother is not helping me.)*

Like **mir**, **dir** is also dative. If you think of the pronoun **du** as being nominative, then the dative form of that pronoun would be **dir**. Observe the chart below.

124

NOMINATIVE (SUBJ./PRED. NOM.)	du
ACCUSATIVE (DIRECT OBJECT)	
DATIVE (INDIRECT OBJECT)	(dir)

Dir is the dative way to say *you*, so as an indirect object it can mean *to you* or *for you*. Or it can be used with verbs that take the dative case, such as **ich helfe**.

Here are a couple of examples of how you could use **dir** in a sentence:

- **Mein Bruder kauft dir ein Geschenk.** *(My brother is buying you a gift.)*
- **Meine Freundinnen helfen dir.** *(My* (female) *friends are helping you.)*

As you can see from the examples, dative pronouns follow the verb.

EXERCISES

1. **Ich helfe dir jeden Tag.**
2. **Meine Mutter hilft mir jeden Tag.**
3. **Wir kaufen dir ein Auto.**
4. **Meine Mutter kauft mir ein Handy.**
5. **Sie kaufen ihrem Sohn ein Auto, aber wir haben kein Geld.**
6. **Mein Hund hilft mir.**
7. **Ihr gebt euren Hunden und Katzen jeden Tag Futter.**
8. **Wir brauchen eine Zeitung.**
9. **Ich kaufe seiner Mutter eine Zeitung.**
10. **Ich gebe den Kindern jede Woche Bücher.**

Answers on page 199.

LESSON 108

PRONUNCIATION TIP: The *ch* in the word **spreche** isn't a scraping sound, but similar to the whooshing sound found in the word **ich**.

Our new verb for this lesson is a stem-changing verb. The "real" stem for this verb is **sprech-**, which you can see is the stem in the first person singular, first person plural, second person plural, and third person plural. But the second person singular and third person singular deviate from this stem and instead have the stem **sprich-**. These two forms are circled in the chart below.

	SINGULAR	PLURAL
FIRST PERSON	ich spreche	wir sprechen
SECOND PERSON	du sprichst	ihr sprecht
THIRD PERSON	er/sie/es spricht	sie sprechen

In order to translate the exercises for this lesson, there are two important words you will need to know: First, **Englisch**, which is the German word for *English*. Also, **Deutsch**, which is the German word for *German*. **Deutsch** sounds sort of like *doych*.

126

EXERCISES

1. **Ich spreche Deutsch.**
2. **Die Kinder geben ihren Müttern ein Geschenk.**
3. **Meine Schwester spricht jeden Tag Deutsch, aber meine Brüder sprechen Englisch.**
4. **Ich spreche Deutsch, aber meine Töchter sprechen Englisch.**
5. **Eure Eltern geben den Kindern Geschenke.**
6. **Meine Mutter spricht Deutsch, aber meine Schwestern sprechen Englisch.**
7. **Meine Mutter kauft mir Geschenke.**
8. **Wir helfen den Kindern.**
9. **Mein Bruder kauft seiner Tochter ein Handy.**
10. **Wir brauchen Essen, aber wir haben kein Geld.**

Answers on page 200.

LESSON 109

NEW WORD   **ich lese**

MEANING   *I read*

PRONUNCIATION TIP: The *s* in **lese** sounds like a *z*, so it sounds something like *LAY-zuh*. The second and third person singular form **liest** sounds like the English word *least*.

Ich lese is yet another stem-changing verb. The stem for this verb is **les-**, but the second person singular and third person singular deviate from this stem and instead have the stem **lies-**.

	SINGULAR	PLURAL
FIRST PERSON	ich lese	wir lesen
SECOND PERSON	(du liest)	ihr lest
THIRD PERSON	(er/sie/es liest)	sie lesen

Here's something to take note of—notice that for this verb, the stems **les-** and **lies-** both end with the letter *s*. So in the second person singular, if we added the personal ending **-st** to the stem, here is what would happen:

lies + st = liesst

Since the stem ends with an *s* and the personal ending begins with an *s*, that would give us the letter *s* twice—so we drop one *s* and we end up with **liest** as the second person singular. This means that the second person singular and third person singular are really the same word: **liest**.

EXERCISES

1. **Ich lese jede Woche zwei Bücher.**
2. **Meine Schwester liest jeden Tag drei Bücher!**
3. **Das Mädchen liest sein Buch.**
4. **Sie lesen die Bücher nicht.**
5. **Ich kaufe dir ein Buch.**
6. **Du liest jeden Tag Bücher.**
7. **Meine Tochter und ihre Freundinnen lesen jede Woche vier Bücher.**
8. **Mein Bruder spricht kein Deutsch, aber er spricht Englisch.**
9. **Sie helfen mir jede Woche.**
10. **Ihr gebt den Kindern Handys.**

Answers on page 200.

LESSON 110

I LIKE TO...

In this lesson you will learn how to say that you like to do a certain activity, like this sentence:

> I like to read.

In German, this kind of sentence is worded differently. Here is how it would be worded if it were a German sentence.

> I read gladly.

In German, the word that means *gladly* is **gern** or **gerne** (they are spelled differently, but they mean exactly the same thing). Here's how we can use **gern** in a German sentence.

> **Ich lese gern.**

A word-for-word translation would say *I read gladly*, but we will translate this kind of sentence into English as *I like to read.*

WORD ORDER WITH "GERN"

When you use the word **gern** to say that you like to do something, you must (as always in German) pay attention to word order—that is, where you should place the word **gern** in the structure of the sentence.

If the sentence has a direct object, put **gern** before the direct object, like this.

> **Ich lese <u>gern</u> Bücher**. *(I like to read books.)*

If the sentence has an indirect object, put **gern** after the indirect object, like this.

> **Ich helfe meinem Vater <u>gern</u>.** (I like to help my father.)

If the sentence has both an indirect object and a direct object, put **gern** after the indirect object but before the direct object, like this.

Meine Schwester kauft ihrem Sohn <u>gern</u> Geschenke. *(My sister likes to buy her son gifts.)*

To say that you don't like to do something, put the word **nicht** right before **gern**, wherever **gern** might happen to be, as in these examples.

- **Ich lese <u>nicht gern</u>.** *(I do not like to read.)*
- **Ich lese <u>nicht gern</u> Bücher.** *(I do not like to read books.)*
- **Ich helfe meinem Vater <u>nicht gern</u>.** *(I do not like to help my father.)*
- **Meine Schwester kauft ihrem Sohn <u>nicht gern</u> Geschenke.** *(My sister does not like to buy her son gifts.)*

The word **gern** can be moved around in the sentence to create different shades of meaning, but in this book we will only work with simple sentence such as the ones shown above.

EXERCISES

1. **Mein Vater liest gern jeden Morgen Zeitung.**
2. **Wir geben unserem Bruder nicht gern Geld.**
3. **Seine Eltern geben den Kindern gern Geschenke.**
4. **Du liest gern Bücher, aber dein Bruder liest nicht gern.**
5. **Mein Bruder hilft mir gern.**
6. **Meine Schwester kauft ihren Freundinnen gern Geschenke.**
7. **Ich spreche gern Deutsch, aber meine Freundinnen sprechen gern Englisch.**
8. **Wir geben dir das Handy.**
9. **Ich kaufe nicht gern Zeitungen.**
10. **Meine Freundin gibt ihrem Sohn ihr Auto und mein Vater gibt mir sein Auto.**

Answers on page 200.

LESSON 111

NEW WORD   **immer / nie**

MEANING   *always / never*

PRONUNCIATION TIP: **Nie** sounds like the English word *knee.*

The words **immer** and **nie** are adverbs. In a German sentence, **immer** and **nie** will generally go after an indirect object but before a direct object.

EXERCISES

1. **Wir sprechen immer Deutsch, aber Thomas und Marina sprechen nie Deutsch.**
2. **Meine Freunde haben immer Geld, aber sie geben mir nie Geld.**
3. **Du kaufst deinem Hund jeden Tag Futter.**
4. **Ihr gebt den Kindern Geschenke.**
5. **Ich kaufe dir jede Woche Essen.**
6. **Wir helfen den Kindern, aber wir geben den Kindern kein Geld.**
7. **Ihr kauft den Müttern und Vätern Geschenke.**
8. **Mein Sohn liest gern Bücher, aber ich lese nie Bücher.**
9. **Mein Hund hat dein Buch nicht.**
10. **Ihre Kinder haben Hunger. Meine Kinder haben auch Hunger.**

Answers on page 200.

LESSON 112

NEW WORD   **ich mag**

MEANING   *I like*

A couple of lessons ago, you learned how to say that you like to do a certain activity. We used the word **gern** to accomplish this.

But you still don't know how to say that you like a noun—that is, a certain person, place, or thing. In order to say that you like a thing or person, use our new verb for this lesson. Observe the various forms of **ich mag** in the chart below.

	SINGULAR	PLURAL
FIRST PERSON	**ich mag**	**wir mögen**
SECOND PERSON	**du magst**	**ihr mögt**
THIRD PERSON	**er/sie/es mag**	**sie mögen**

Let's take a look at how you can use **ich mag** in a sentence. Let's say, for instance, that you want to say that you like books. Here is how you would say it:

Ich mag Bücher. *(I like books.)*

EXERCISES

1. **Ich mag dein Handy.**
2. **Du magst Bücher, aber ich lese nicht gern.**
3. **Meine Schwestern mögen dein Auto nicht, aber ich mag dein Auto.**
4. **Meine Kinder mögen keine Katzen—sie mögen Hunde.**
5. **Ich spreche gern Deutsch, aber mein Sohn spricht immer Englisch.**

6. **Meine Schwestern kaufen dir ein Geschenk.**
7. **Wir sprechen jeden Tag Deutsch.**
8. **Meine Eltern kaufen mir ein Auto, aber sie haben kein Geld.**
9. **Du kaufst den Hunden Futter, aber sie brauchen kein Futter.**
10. **Ich helfe meinen Schwestern immer, aber meine Schwestern helfen mir nie.**

Answers on page 200.

LESSON 113

PREPOSITIONS

A preposition is a word that shows a relationship or connection between two nouns. Examples of prepositions are *in, below, above,* and *beside.* Here's an example of a sentence with a preposition.

> The bicycle is inside the garage.

In that sentence, the word *inside* is the preposition. Notice that in this sentence there are two items being talked about: the bicycle and the garage. The preposition showed the relationship between the two items.

The person saying this sentence wants to tell someone about the location of the bicycle. I suppose the speaker could have indicated the location of the bicycle a different way—if the speaker happened to be near the bicycle, he or she could have pointed at it and said, "It's over here," or "It's over there." But with a preposition, you don't have to be near the object you want to talk about, because you can show its location just with words by using something else as a point of reference.

Let's look at that sentence again and observe how the speaker used the garage as a point of reference.

The bicycle is inside the garage.

The speaker uses the garage as a point of reference to show where the bicycle was. The preposition *inside* referred directly to the garage. In grammatical terms, the word that the preposition refers to is called the *object of the preposition.*

Therefore, in our example sentence, the word *inside* is the preposition and the word *garage* is the object of the preposition.

Just for practice, in each of the following sentences, see if you can spot the preposition and the object of the preposition.

EXERCISES

1. Your book fell behind the couch.
2. Just put that plant beside the lamp.
3. The spare tire is in the trunk.
4. The car is going through the tunnel.
5. I just saw a chipmunk run under the house!
6. I want to get this done before lunch.
7. After school, the accordion ensemble will rehearse again.
8. The new store is by the post office.
9. You aren't allowed to do that on campus.
10. Have you ever wondered what is beyond that mountain?

Answers on page 201.

LESSON 114

NEW WORD   **mit**

MEANING   *with*

In the last lesson, you learned about prepositions, and in this lesson you are learning your first German preposition. In German, prepositions don't work alone—they work in conjunction mainly with one of two cases: the accusative case and the dative case. When you see a German preposition, the object of that preposition must be in one of those cases.

Whenever you learn a new German preposition, you must remember what case that particular preposition uses. For example, **mit**, our new word for this lesson, uses the dative case. Therefore, the object of the preposition **mit** must always be in the dative case.

You may use **mit** as you would the English word *with.* Here are some examples of how you can use the preposition **mit** with the dative case.

- **Ich lese gern mit meinen Kindern Bücher.** *(I like to read books with my children.)*
- **Meine Mutter spricht Deutsch mit ihren Eltern.** *(My mother speaks German with her parents.)*
- **Mein Sohn spricht Deutsch mit mir, aber er spricht Englisch mit dir.** *(My son speaks German with me, but he speaks English with you.)*

EXERCISES
1. **Frau Smith liest gern jede Woche mit unseren Kindern Bücher.**
2. **Du sprichst gern Deutsch mit mir.**
3. **Sie spricht jeden Tag Englisch mit ihren Brüdern.**
4. **Ich spreche jede Woche Deutsch mit dir, aber ich spreche nicht gern Deutsch.**
5. **Ihr sprecht nie Englisch mit mir—ihr sprecht immer Deutsch.**
6. **Wir lesen gern jeden Tag die Zeitung.**
7. **Mein Freund kauft ein Handy.**
8. **Der Junge mag Hunde, aber er hat eine Katze.**
9. **Wir lesen gern mit unseren Freunden Bücher.**
10. **Sie kaufen mir nie Bücher.**

Answers on page 201.

LESSON 115

NEW WORD   **über**

MEANING   *about*

PRONUNCIATION TIP: Pronounce the beginning of the word **über** with rounded lips, so it sounds something like *OOOH-bah*.

Our new word for this lesson is a preposition. As we mentioned before, each preposition must work along with a certain case. The preposition **über**, our new word for this lesson, must take the accusative case.

Here's how to use the word **über**. Let's say that you want to make a statement like this one:

I would like to talk about my dog.

In German, the part that says *about my dog* would be this:

über meinen Hund

Notice that **meinen** is accusative because the preposition **über** takes the accusative case.

EXERCISES

1. **Ich kaufe ein Buch über Katzen.**
2. **Mein Bruder hat ein Buch über Autos, aber er hat kein Auto.**
3. **Wir sprechen über unseren Hund—er hat kein Wasser.**
4. **Wir lesen gern jeden Tag die Zeitung, aber sie lesen nie die Zeitung.**
5. **Er kauft mir eine Zeitung.**
6. **Ihr sprecht nicht gern Englisch, aber wir sprechen jeden Tag Englisch.**
7. **Wir geben den Jungen und Mädchen jede Woche Geld.**
8. **Mein Bruder hat fünf Dollar, aber er gibt mir nicht gern Geld.**
9. **Meine Freunde mögen Autos, aber ich mag Bücher.**
10. **Wir brauchen ein Auto, aber wir haben kein Geld.**

Answers on page 201.

LESSON 116

NEW WORD   **für**

MEANING   *for*

PRONUNCIATION TIP: **Für** does not sound like the English word *fur* (like the fur on a cat). **Für** has a *yuh* sound after the *f* at the beginning of the word, so it sounds something like *fyure*.

Für is a preposition that takes the accusative case. You can use it in some of the same ways that you would use the word *for* in English.

So far, you know how to say that you are buying something for someone or giving something to someone using the dative case, like this:

> **Ich kaufe meiner Mutter ein Geschenk.** *(I am buying my mother a gift.)*

But you can say the exact same thing in German using the preposition **für**, like this:

> **Ich kaufe ein Geschenk für meine Mutter.** *(I am buying a gift for my mother.)*

These two sentences say the same thing, and they are both correct. The main difference is word order. When you say **für meine Mutter**, you have to put that prepositional phrase after the direct object.

This is an example of one of those times when being a native English speaker can give you a nice advantage when learning German, because in English we say sentences with the exact same word order as both of the examples we showed you above. Observe these sentences:

- I am buying my mother a gift.
- I am buying a gift for my mother.

Since we use the same word order in English, saying German sentences like these may feel natural to you.

137

1. **Ich kaufe ein Auto für meinen Sohn.**
2. **Frau Johnson kauft ein Geschenk für ihren Mann.**
3. **Wir haben kein Geld, aber wir kaufen Handys für unsere Kinder.**
4. **Wir mögen Bücher und wir lesen immer Bücher mit unseren Kindern.**
5. **Ihr sprecht Englisch, aber wir sprechen Deutsch.**
6. **Frau Smith kauft ihren Hunden jede Woche Futter.**
7. **Frau Smith kauft jede Woche Futter für ihre Hunde.**
8. **Der Junge liest gern Bücher über Katzen.**
9. **Ich spreche nie Deutsch mit dir.**
10. **Du gibst deinem Vater immer Geld.**

Answers on page 201.

LESSON 117

NEW WORD **mich / dich**

MEANING *me / you*

PRONUNCIATION TIP: The *ch* in **mich** and **dich** sounds like the beginning of the word *huge*.

You already know the dative form of the pronouns *me* and *you*: **mir** and **dir**. Now, in this lesson we want to show you the accusative forms of those same pronouns. They are **mich** and **dich**. Observe these charts:

NOMINATIVE (SUBJ./PRED. NOM.)	ich
ACCUSATIVE (DIRECT OBJECT)	mich
DATIVE (INDIRECT OBJECT)	mir

NOMINATIVE (SUBJ./PRED. NOM.)	du
ACCUSATIVE (DIRECT OBJECT)	dich
DATIVE (INDIRECT OBJECT)	dir

Since **mich** and **dich** are in the accusative case, you can use them with prepositions that take the accusative case, like this:

- **Mein Freund kauft ein Geschenk für mich.** *(My friend is buying a gift for me.)*
- **Meine Eltern sprechen über dich.** *(My parents are talking about you.)*

EXERCISES

1. **Ich kaufe dir ein Geschenk.**
2. **Ich kaufe ein Geschenk für dich.**
3. **Du kaufst mir ein Geschenk.**
4. **Du kaufst ein Geschenk für mich.**
5. **Deine Mutter spricht Deutsch, aber dein Vater spricht Englisch.**
6. **Ich mag dich, aber du magst mich nicht.**
7. **Meine Tochter mag keine Katzen.**
8. **Die Jungen haben ein Geschenk für dich.**
9. **Mein Hund mag sein Futter.**
10. **Mein Freund gibt seiner Tochter nicht gern sein Handy.**

Answers on page 201.

LESSON 118

ASKING QUESTIONS IN GERMAN

Questions are an important part of any conversation. Fortunately for us, it is very easy to ask questions in German. Imagine the following sentence:

Du sprichst Englisch. *(You speak English.)*

To turn this into a question, all you have to do is switch the subject and the verb, like this:

Sprichst du Englisch? *(Do you speak English?)*

This technique of switching the subject and verb is called *inversion*.

After you translate the following exercises, see if you can make up some questions on your own just for practice.

EXERCISES

1. **Sprichst du gern Englisch mit deinen Freundinnen?**
2. **Magst du mich?**
3. **Hat Frau Johnson einen Hund?**
4. **Kaufst du meinem Sohn ein Geschenk?**
5. **Habt ihr eine Katze?**
6. **Ist sie deine Freundin?**
7. **Hast du Futter und Wasser für deinen Hund?**
8. **Hat deine Tochter ein Handy?**
9. **Meine Eltern sprechen über die Kinder.**
10. **Meine Freunde kaufen mir nie Geschenke.**

Answers on page 202.

LESSON 119

NEW WORD   **ja / nein**

MEANING   *yes / no*

Now that you know how to ask questions, you need to know how to answer them.
Ja means *yes*. It sounds like *yah*. **Nein** means *no*. It sounds like the English word
nine.

EXERCISES

1. **Kaufst du jeden Tag Essen?**
2. **Nein, ich kaufe jede Woche Essen.**
3. **Hat dein Bruder ein Kind?**
4. **Ja, mein Bruder hat drei Töchter.**
5. **Haben die Männer ein Geschenk für mich?**
6. **Ja, die Männer haben ein Geschenk für dich.**
7. **Bist du eine Mutter?**
8. **Nein, ich bin keine Mutter.**
9. **Lest ihr gern Bücher mit euren Kindern?**
10. **Ja, wir lesen jeden Tag Bücher.**

Answers on page 202.

LESSON 120

TWO-WAY PREPOSITIONS

By now you have some good experience working with prepositions. You know that in German, a preposition must work only with either the accusative case or dative case. Some prepositions, such as **mit**, take the dative case. Other prepositions, such as **über** and **für**, take the accusative case.

But in German there are some special prepositions called *two-way prepositions*. These prepositions can take either the dative case or the accusative case. Not only that, these prepositions can mean different things depending on what case they take. For example, one German preposition **in** can mean *at* when it takes the dative case, and *to* when it takes the accusative case.

In the next lesson, we will start working with a two-way preposition, and we will learn how to use it in a different way with each case.

LESSON 121

NEW WORD   **in**

MEANING   *to* (when it takes the accusative)

In the last lesson, you learned about two-way prepositions. You learned that a two-way preposition is a preposition that can take either the dative case or the accusative case. And, a two-way preposition means a different thing with each case.

In this lesson, we are learning our first two-way preposition. The preposition **in** can take either the dative case or the accusative case. In this lesson, however, we are only going to study how it works with the accusative case.

When **in** takes the accusative case, it means *to*. We would like to show you some examples of sentences using **in**—but so far you don't know any words for places to go. So, let's learn a few new words so that when you use the word **in**, you'll have somewhere to go. Most people go to the store, to school, and to the movie theater, so let's learn how to say those words in German.

142

The most common word for *store* in German is **Supermarkt. Supermarkt** is masculine. The German word for *school* is **Schule**, which is feminine (it sounds something like *SHOO-leh)*. The word for *movie theater* is **Kino**, which is a neuter noun. **Kino** is related to the English word *cinema*.

Now that we have some places to go, let's use the word **in** in a couple of short examples. Remember that **in** is a two-way preposition, and it only means *to* when it takes the accusative case, so for now we will only use it with the accusative case.

Here's an example with the masculine noun **Supermarkt**.

in den Supermarkt *(to the store)*

And here's one with the feminine noun **Schule**.

in die Schule *(to school)*

That leaves us with the neuter noun **Kino**. Since **Kino** is neuter, we need to use the neuter definite article **das** with it. Here's what we would like to say:

in das Kino *(to the cinema)*

But there's a complication! When the preposition **in** comes right before **das**, these two words combine into the word **ins**. So really, the example above is not correct. Here's how it would be written correctly:

ins Kino *(to the cinema)*

So remember this formula:

in + das = ins

In does not combine with any **ein** words, so they stay the same.

REGIONAL VARIATIONS

Although Germany is a bit smaller than the state of Texas, there are many regional variations in the way the German language is spoken throughout Germany. Furthermore, there are dialectical differences in neighboring countries such as Austria and Switzerland. For this reason, some German native German speakers may prefer to use the preposition **zu** (pronounced *tsu*) instead of **in**, as we have here in this lesson. This could be because of where someone grew up, how their parents spoke the language, or any number of reasons. So as you learn, be aware that there may be other ways to say the same thing in German—and sometimes Germans disagree over what is correct and what is not!

LESSON 122

NEW WORD   **ich gehe**

MEANING   *I go*

Now that you know how to use the preposition **in** with the accusative case, you're really going places! But we need a verb to help us get wherever we are going.

In German, to say that you are going somewhere, you need the verb **ich gehe**. Observe the different forms of this verb in this handy chart.

	SINGULAR	PLURAL
FIRST PERSON	**ich gehe**	**wir gehen**
SECOND PERSON	**du gehst**	**ihr geht**
THIRD PERSON	**er/sie/es geht**	**sie gehen**

EXERCISES

1. **Ich gehe jede Woche mit meinen Freundinnen ins Kino.**
2. **Gehen deine Eltern jeden Tag in den Supermarkt?**
3. **Nein, sie gehen jede Woche in den Supermarkt.**
4. **Meine Schwester geht jede Woche in die Schule.**
5. **Kaufst du mir ein Geschenk?**
6. **Ich gehe immer mit meinem Bruder in die Schule.**
7. **Ihr lest nie Bücher über Geld.**
8. **Wir haben ein Geschenk für dich.**
9. **Die Mädchen gehen in den Supermarkt, aber sie haben kein Geld.**
10. **Sie gehen gern mit ihren Kindern ins Kino.**

Answers on page 202.

LESSON 123

NEW WORD   **jetzt / heute**

MEANING   *now / today*

PRONUNCIATION TIP: The *j* in **jetzt** sounds like a *y*, so **jetzt** sounds like *yetst*. **Heute** sounds like *HOY-tuh*.

EXERCISES

1. **Meine Brüder gehen jetzt mit ihren Freunden ins Kino.**
2. **Geht mein Sohn heute in die Schule?**
3. **Meine Söhne lesen heute ein Buch über Hunde und Katzen.**
4. **Die Jungen kaufen ein Geschenk für ihren Hund.**
5. **Meine Freundinnen gehen mit ihren Kindern in den Supermarkt.**
6. **Wir sprechen über unsere Kinder.**
7. **Ich mag Alex nicht, aber ich mag sein Auto.**
8. **Gehen unsere Töchter gern jede Woche ins Kino?**
9. **Ja, und sie gehen heute mit ihren Freundinnen ins Kino.**
10. **Die Jungen kaufen mir ein Geschenk.**

Answers on page 202.

LESSON 124

TIME, MANNER, PLACE

In the past few lessons you have learned how to add more detail to a German sentence by describing the timing of an activity, the place of an activity, and other circumstances such as whether or not the activity will be with this person or that person. As we explained way back in lesson 105, the words and phrases that tell when, how, and where the action is happening are called *adverbs* or *adverbial phrases*. In German, adverbs and adverbial phrases must go in a particular order, and that order is what this lesson is all about.

Imagine that you are going to the movies, and you need to tell your family where you are going. There will probably be several details that you will need to share with them before you leave the house. You might say things like this:

- When you are going
- With whom are you going
- Where you are going

In short, you'll want to tell them the timing of the activity, the circumstances surrounding the activity, and the place of the activity. We can classify these statements into three categories like this:

- Time
- Manner
- Place

Imagine for a moment that you wanted to say it all in one big sentence—what would you put first? What you would put second? Which of the following sentences sounds natural to you?

1. I'm going to the movies with my friends now.
2. I'm going to the movies now with my friends.
3. I'm going with my friends to the movies now.
4. I'm going with my friends now to the movies.
5. I'm going now to the movies with my friends.

146

6. I'm going now with my friends to the movies.

In everyday conversation, although any of the above sentences will work just fine, some might sound better or more natural than others. But they are all still considered acceptable English, and they all do a fine job of communicating their intended meaning. Each of these sentences communicates to the listener the time, manner, and place of the activity.

But if you are a student of German, you can't just put these adverbs and adverbial phrases in whatever order you want. Instead, there is a guiding principle that helps students know how to arrange adverbs and adverbial phrases in a sentence. Here it is:

$$\boxed{\text{TIME} \cdot \text{MANNER} \cdot \text{PLACE}}$$

Say it over and over so you can remember it: time, manner, place. Time, manner, place. This is the order you should try to follow when formulating a German sentence. When you are composing a sentence, you'll want to mention the timing of the activity first, then the manner in which you will do the activity, then finally the place of the activity.

So let's try this out in German. If we follow this rule, we will want to word a German sentence like this:

I'm going <u>now</u> <u>with my friends</u> <u>to the movies</u>.
　　　　　TIME　　MANNER　　　PLACE

Here's how that would look in German:

Ich gehe <u>jetzt</u> <u>mit meinen Freunden</u> <u>ins Kino</u>.
　　　　　　TIME　　　　MANNER　　　　　PLACE

Jetzt tells the timing, **mit meinen Freunden** tells the manner or circumstances of the activity, and **ins Kino** tells the place.

If a sentence doesn't include all three elements, that's fine—just keep the information you include in the same order as before. This sentence, for example, only has time and manner:

Ich gehe jetzt mit meinen Freunden. *(I am going now with my friends.)*

This one just has time and place:

Ich gehe jetzt ins Kino. *(I am going now to the movies.)*

This one only has manner and place:

Ich gehe mit meinen Freunden ins Kino. *(I am going with my friends to the movies.)*

If you continue to study German (and we hope you do), this concept will become more and more important because you will learn more vocabulary that can be used to describe times and places. Also, you will learn exceptions to this rule. But in the meantime, remember always: *time, manner, place!*

LESSON 125

NEW WORD **Einkaufszentrum**

MEANING *mall, shopping center*

Einkaufszentrum is a neuter noun. It can mean *mall* or *shopping center*, but in this book we will just use it to mean *mall*.

As you work through the following exercises, try to identify any adverbs or adverbial phrases. As you do, check to make sure that they are organized according to the special order you learned about in the last lesson: *time, manner, place.*

EXERCISES

1. **Wir gehen jede Woche ins Einkaufszentrum, aber sie gehen nie ins Einkaufszentrum.**
2. **Gehen die Jungen heute ins Einkaufszentrum?**
3. **Nein, aber sie gehen jede Woche mit ihren Eltern ins Einskaufszentrum.**
4. **Dein Vater geht nie in die Schule, aber deine Schwester geht jeden Tag in die Schule.**
5. **Meine Frau liest mit unseren Kindern ein Buch.**
6. **Wir mögen Autos und ich lese heute ein Buch über Autos.**
7. **Ich spreche jeden Tag mit meiner Schwester, aber ich spreche nicht jeden Tag mit mit meinem Bruder.**
8. **Geht deine Mutter heute mit dir in den Supermarkt?**
9. **Kaufst du heute ein Geschenk für mich?**
10. **Gehst du heute mit mir ins Einkaufszentrum?**

Answers on page 202.

LESSON 126

NEW WORD   **Park / Bibliothek**

MEANING   *park / library*

Park is masculine. The plural form is **Parks**.

Bibliothek is feminine. The plural form is **Bibliotheken**.

Whenever you see multiple adverbs or adverbial phrases in an exercise, try to figure out the order in which they are organized. Are they arranged in the order of *time, manner, place?*

EXERCISES

1. **Arnold geht heute mit seinen Hunden in den Park.**
2. **Geht ihr heute mit euren Kindern in den Park?**
3. **Sie gehen nie in den Park, aber ihre Söhne gehen jeden Tag mit ihren Hunden in den Park.**
4. **Mein Sohn liest nicht gern Bücher, aber er geht jeden Tag in die Bibliothek.**
5. **Wir sprechen immer Deutsch, aber meine Eltern sprechen nie Deutsch.**
6. **Ich kaufe heute Futter für meine Hunde.**
7. **Sie kaufen dem Mädchen ein Geschenk.**
8. **Sprecht ihr über unseren Hund?**
9. **Ja, wir sprechen über euren Hund.**
10. **Ich helfe dir. Hilfst du mir?**

Answers on page 203.

LESSON 127

NEW WORD   **oft / selten**

MEANING   *often / seldom*

EXERCISES

1. **Du gehst oft mit deinem Hund in den Park, aber du gehst selten mit mir in den Park.**
2. **Du gehst nicht oft in den Supermarkt, aber ich gehe jeden Tag in den Supermarkt.**
3. **Ich gehe selten ins Einkaufszentrum, aber ich gehe jede Woche in die Bibliothek.**
4. **Geht ihr jetzt mit euren Freunden ins Kino?**
5. **Gehen deine Schwestern oft mit dir ins Einkaufszentrum?**
6. **Nein, meine Schwestern gehen nie mit mir ins Einkaufszentrum, aber sie gehen jeden Tag mit ihren Freundinnen.**
7. **Meine Eltern kaufen dir ein Geschenk, aber sie kaufen kein Geschenk für mich.**
8. **Wir haben deine Bücher und wir gehen jetzt in die Bibliothek.**
9. **Ihr Sohn geht heute in die Schule, aber mein Sohn geht heute nicht in die Schule.**
10. **Unsere Freunde gehen heute mit ihren Kindern und Hunden in den Park, aber sie mögen den Park nicht.**

Answers on page 203.

LESSON 128

NEW WORD   **ohne**

MEANING   *without*

Ohne is a preposition that takes the accusative case.

EXERCISES

1. **Sie geht nie ohne ihr Geld ins Einkaufszentrum.**
2. **Wir gehen selten in den Park, aber unser Freund Peter geht jeden Tag.**
3. **Sie gehen nie ohne ihre Bücher in die Bibliothek.**
4. **Kaufst du ein Geschenk für meinen Hund?**
5. **Du liest gern jeden Tag Bücher in der Bibliothek.**
6. **Helga geht jede Woche in die Bibliothek.**
7. **Ich kaufe meinem Vater ein Buch, aber er kauft mir nie Geschenke.**
8. **Deine Schwester mag Bücher, aber sie geht nie in die Bibliothek.**
9. **Das Mädchen hilft gern ihrem Vater, aber es hilft dir nie.**
10. **Gehen wir heute in den Supermarkt?**

Answers on page 203.

LESSON 129

NEW WORD   **in**

MEANING   *in / at* (when it takes the dative)

You already know the preposition **in**. You have used it with the accusative case in a way that means *to*. But that's not all that the preposition **in** can do. As you already know, **in** is a two-way preposition that can take either the accusative case or the dative case. So, now it's time to learn how to use this preposition with the dative case.

When we use **in** with the dative case, it means *in*, meaning inside of something. Observe this example sentence:

Ich bin in der Schule. *(I am inside the school.)*

But usually we don't say that kind of thing in English, unless you want to say specifically that you are inside the school as opposed to standing in front of the school. But generally speaking, if you are inside the school, you would probably say *I am at the school*. Therefore, whenever we give you an exercise that has **in** plus the dative case, we will translate the word **in** in the answer key as *in/at*. This will help you remember that in German, **in** plus the dative means that you are inside something.

So, the German word **in** can be used in two ways: with the accusative case to mean *to*, or with the dative case to mean *in/at*. When you are reading German and you see the word **in**, you can't just assume what it will mean. Instead, you must observe what case **in** is working with so you can figure out what it is communicating.

Another equally good way to determine what **in** means is to look at the verb. If the verb is a verb of being, like **ist**, then the preposition **in** is probably going to mean *in/at* and take the dative case. Likewise, if the verb is a verb of motion, like **gehen**, then the preposition **in** is more likely to mean *to* and take the accusative case. Therefore, as always, when translating, context is your friend.

CONTRACTIONS

You already know that when **in** comes before the definite article **das** those two words merge into the word **ins**. Well, the same thing happens when **in** takes the dative case. Here's an example with **in** plus a masculine noun.

> **Ich bin <u>in dem</u> Supermarkt.** *(I am in/at the store.)*

But **in** and **dem** merge into the word **im**, so it ends up looking like this:

> **Ich bin <u>im</u> Supermarkt.** *(I am in/at the store.)*

So remember this formula:

> **in + dem = im**

If you keep studying German, in the future you will see more examples of prepositions that merge with the definite article. But prepositions will not merge with any form of **ein**, or any **ein** words, so you don't have to worry about that.

EXERCISES

1. **Wir sind oft in der Schule.**
2. **Sie sind mit ihren Freunden im Park.**
3. **Seid ihr mit den Kindern in der Bibliothek?**
4. **Wir brauchen ein Geschenk für deinen Vater.**
5. **Mein Mann ist oft mit unseren Kindern in der Bibliothek.**
6. **Wir gehen nie ohne unsere Freundinnen ins Einkaufszentrum.**
7. **Meine Söhne kaufen ihrer Mutter heute ein Geschenk.**
8. **Mein Bruder und seine Kinder gehen ins Einkaufszentrum.**
9. **Meine Frau geht gern mit unseren Kindern ins Kino, aber ich mag das Kino nicht.**
10. **Helfen sie mir heute?**

Answers on page 203.

LESSON 130

NEW WORD   **auf**

MEANING   *on top of / onto*

Auf, our new word for this lesson is yet another two-way preposition. Being a two-way preposition, it can take either the accusative case or the dative case.

When **auf** takes the dative case, it means *on*, like when something is on top of something else. Here's an example:

Das Buch ist auf dem Tisch. *(The book is on the table.)*

When you use **auf** with the accusative case, it means something like the English word *onto*, like in this sentence:

Die Katze geht auf den Tisch. *(The cat is going onto the table.)*

So when **auf** takes the dative case, the object is stationary, just sitting on top of something. But when **auf** takes the accusative case, the idea is that the object is moving onto some kind of surface.

EXERCISES

1. **Der Hund ist auf dem Stuhl.**
2. **Der Hund geht auf den Stuhl.**
3. **Der Stuhl ist auf dem Tisch.**
4. **Sind ihre Bücher auf unserem Tisch?**
5. **Ich habe die Zeitung nicht. Sie ist auf dem Stuhl.**
6. **Ihr seid in der Schule.**
7. **Ihre Mutter und mein Vater sind im Supermarkt.**
8. **Meine Freunde gehen nie ohne Geld ins Kino.**
9. **Meine Schwester geht oft in die Bibliothek, aber wir lesen nie Bücher.**
10. **Ich spreche nie Deutsch mit dir, aber du sprichst immer Deutsch mit mir.**

Answers on page 204.

LESSON 131

NEW WORD **ich will**

MEANING *I want*

Observe the various forms of **ich will** in the chart below. This verb is irregular, so you'll have to memorize the forms.

	Singular	Plural
First Person	**ich will**	**wir wollen**
Second Person	**du willst**	**ihr wollt**
Third Person	**er/sie/es will**	**sie wollen**

EXERCISES

1. **Ich will einen Hund.**
2. **Meine Söhne wollen eine Katze.**
3. **Unser Bruder will mein Geld, aber ich habe kein Geld.**
4. **Will deine Mutter mein Auto?**
5. **Meine Schwester will zehn Dollar.**
6. **Die Hunde wollen Futter.**
7. **Wir wollen ein Auto, aber wir brauchen kein Auto.**
8. **Unsere Tochter braucht ein Auto, aber sie will kein Auto.**
9. **Die Jungen gehen nie ohne ihre Freunde ins Kino.**
10. **Sie mögen dich, aber mögen sie mich?**

Answers on page 204.

LESSON 132

INFINITIVES

An infinitive is the word *to* plus a verb. Here are some examples of infinitives:

- to walk
- to eat
- to run
- to be

Let's examine some of the different ways infinitives are used:

- I like <u>to sing</u>.
- I want <u>to be</u> a teacher.
- <u>To eat</u> a watermelon is sheer delight.
- I am unable <u>to finish</u> my homework.
- I want <u>to play</u> checkers.

Try to locate the infinitive in each of the exercises below. But be careful! A few of the exercises do not have infinitives. Can you tell which ones they are?

EXERCISES

1. I do not like to wash the dishes.
2. They want to play a different game.
3. I went to the store.
4. Charles wants to be a policeman.
5. To forgive is divine.
6. She wants to return that sweater to the store.
7. Jenny would like to play the clarinet.
8. We will not go to the party.
9. She will go to the furniture store to buy a chair.
10. Throw the ball to Jeremy.

Answers on page 204.

LESSON 133

NEW WORD   **kaufen**

MEANING   *to buy*

In English, it takes two words to express an infinitive: the word *to* and a verb. In German, however, it only takes one word to express an infinitive.

In this lesson, we learn our first German infinitive: the word **kaufen**. Notice that the infinitive **kaufen** looks just like the first person plural and third person plural forms of the verb:

- **wir kaufen** *(we buy)*
- **sie kaufen** *(they buy)*
- **kaufen** *(to buy)*

You can use the infinitive **kaufen** along with **ich will**, which we learned only a couple of lessons ago. Here's an example:

    Ich will kaufen... *(I want to buy...)*

Now let's use **kaufen** in a complete sentence:

    Ich will ein Auto kaufen. *(I want to buy a car.)*

Notice that in German, the infinitive goes at the end of the sentence, after the direct object. A word-for-word translation into English would say *I want a car to buy*. Of course, this is different from the way we would do in it English—in English, the infinitive goes right after the main verb.

In the following exercises, get some practice working with the infinitive **kaufen**, and in the next lesson we will learn more about infinitives.

EXERCISES

1. **Ich will jetzt ein Buch kaufen.**
2. **Willst du ein Auto kaufen?**
3. **Meine Schwester will eine Zeitung kaufen.**
4. **Wir wollen Essen kaufen, aber wir haben kein Geld.**
5. **Wollt ihr einen Tisch kaufen?**
6. **Sie wollen Stühle und einen Tisch kaufen.**
7. **Die Zeitung ist immer auf dem Tisch.**
8. **Die Katze geht oft auf den Stuhl.**
9. **Mein Bruder ist jeden Tag im Park.**
10. **Die Jungen gehen gern mit ihren Hunden in den Park.**

Answers on page 204.

LESSON 134

MORE ABOUT INFINITIVES

In the last lesson you learned your first German infinitive which was **kaufen**. But that's not the only German verb that has an infinitive—every verb has one. So now that you have been introduced to infinitives, and you have a little experience working with them, it's time to learn the infinitive forms of some of the other verbs you know. For practice, let's use each one in a sentence. You won't use the infinitive of every verb, but the ones you are likely to need are listed below with examples sentences.

Ich bin means *I am*. It is the verb of being or existing. The infinitive form is **sein**, which means *to be*. (This word looks and sounds just like the word **sein** which means *his* or *its*). It sounds something like *zyne*. Here is a sentence that uses the infinitive **sein**.

    Ich will ein Vater sein. *(I want to be a father.)*

Ich habe means *I have*. The infinitive form is **haben** which means *to have*. Here is a sentence that uses the infinitive **haben**.

> **Ich will einen Hund haben.** *(I want to have a dog.)*

Ich gebe means *I give*. The infinitive form is **geben** which means *to give*. Here is a sentence that uses the infinitive **geben**.

> **Ich will dir ein Geschenk geben.** *(I want to give you a gift.)*

Ich helfe means *I help*. The infinitive form is **helfen** which means *to help*. Here is a sentence that uses the infinitive **helfen**.

> **Ich will dir nicht helfen.** *(I don't want to help you.)*

Ich spreche means *I speak* or *I talk*. The infinitive form is **sprechen** which means *to speak* or *to talk*. Here is a sentence that uses the infinitive **sprechen**.

> **Er will über Katzen sprechen.** *(He wants to talk about cats.)*

Ich lese means *I read*. The infinitive form is **lesen** which means *to read*. Here is a sentence that uses the infinitive **lesen**.

> **Ihr wollt ein Buch über Katzen lesen.** *(Y'all want to read a book about cats.)*

In this lesson, we have thrown a lot of new words at you—the infinitive of each verb. Keep working with these infinitives and reading the practice sentences in this lesson repeatedly until you are comfortable with all of them. Over the next few lessons, you'll learn even more verbs that you can use infinitives with.

LESSON 135

NEW WORD   **ich kann**

MEANING   *I am able / I can*

PRONUNCIATION TIP: Notice that some forms of this verb have an *o* with an **Umlaut**. That sounds like the *e* in bed, but pronounced with rounded lips—so it will sound something like *KUHR-nen*.

Use this chart to study the various forms of **ich kann**, our new verb for this lesson.

	SINGULAR	PLURAL
FIRST PERSON	**ich kann**	**wir können**
SECOND PERSON	**du kannst**	**ihr könnt**
THIRD PERSON	**er/sie/es kann**	**sie können**

In German, we use the verb **ich kann** to say that we are able to do something. But **ich kann** cannot do anything by itself. It needs an infinitive to complete its meaning. Observe the following examples:

- **Ich kann ein Auto kaufen.** (*I am able to buy a car* OR *I can buy a car.*)
- **Ich kann in den Supermarkt gehen.** (*I am able to go to the store* OR *I can go to the store.*)

To say that you can't do something, you'll need some kind of way to negate the sentence. There are two possible ways to do it, depending on if a definite article is involved, or if an indefinite article is involved.

If you are saying that you can't do an activity that pertains to a noun with a definite article, here is how you would word it:

161

Ich kann nicht in die Bibliothek gehen. *(I am not able to go to the library* OR *I cannot go to the library.)*

Notice that in that example, the word **Bibliothek** was preceded by a definite article, so it was *the* library (not just any ol' library).

If you are saying that you can't do an activity that pertains to a noun with an indefinite article, here is how you would word it:

Ich kann kein Auto kaufen. *(I am not able to buy a car* OR *I cannot buy a car.)*

Notice that in that example, the word **Auto** was preceded by an indefinite article. Therefore it was not any particular car, but just some car. That kind of sentence will be negated by using **kein** along with a noun.

EXERCISES

1. **Ich kann ins Einkaufszentrum gehen, aber wir können nicht in den Supermarkt gehen.**
2. **Meine Hunde können nicht in die Bibliothek gehen.**
3. **Deine Schwester will ins Einkaufszentrum gehen, aber sie kann nicht gehen.**
4. **Die Katze ist immer auf dem Tisch.**
5. **Ihr Hund kann nicht in den Park gehen.**
6. **Wir können in die Schule gehen.**
7. **Die Katze geht gern auf den Tisch.**
8. **Die Mädchen wollen ins Einkaufszentrum gehen, aber wir haben kein Geld.**
9. **Meine Töchter gehen nie ohne ihr Geld in den Supermarkt.**
10. **Meine Eltern sind in der Schule.**

Answers on page 204.

LESSON 136

FORMAL AND INFORMAL SPEECH

If you met the queen of England, would you speak to her the same way as you would speak to your friends? Probably not!

With your friends, you would probably speak informally—perhaps using slang words or other types of speech that close friends or family typically use with one another. However, if you met someone important, or a stranger, or someone older than you, you would probably speak in a more formal way. In the German language, there is certain way to speak to others that is considered more formal than the usual way of speaking. To help explain this more formal way of speaking, let's use our imagination a little.

Imagine for a moment that you are in a palace in England. The queen's butler is in the kitchen, taking a break. The cook, who is also taking a break, sits nearby sipping a cup of coffee. The butler says to his friend the cook, "You usually drink tea."

Later that same day, the queen asks for some coffee. The butler says to the queen, "Your Majesty usually drinks tea."

Go back and reread each of the butler's statements, paying special attention to the subject and the verb of each sentence. What differences do you notice?

Many lessons ago, we learned about a certain quality that verbs have called *person*. First person, second person, and third person are three different aspects or relationships with the speaker that a given verb can have. When the butler asked the cook if he wanted another cup of tea, the butler spoke to him as you would expect—in the second person, like this:

> <u>You</u> usually <u>drink</u> tea.

Since the butler was the cook's friend and colleague, he spoke to him in a way that people would ordinarily speak to one another—using the word *you* along with the second person verb *drink*. But do you think it would be acceptable for the butler to speak to the queen in the same way that he would address a friend or fellow worker? No. Instead, our imaginary butler spoke to the queen like this:

Your Majesty usually <u>drinks</u> tea.

In this example, the butler addressed the queen in a formal way—using the special title *Your Majesty*, along with the third person verb *drinks*. If the butler had addressed the queen in the same way as he addressed the cook, with the word *you*, it might have sounded out of place—too informal to show the proper level of respect that is appropriate for a queen.

Likewise, in a courtroom, you would not address the judge as *you*, but instead you would use a formal title such as *Your Honor*. And again, you would use a third person verb along with that title. In court, you might hear something like this:

<u>Your Honor</u> <u>is</u> welcome to see the document.

If you met a high-ranking politician from another country, you might refer to him or her with the title *Your Excellency*, again, with a third person verb.

So by now, you get the point—in English, to address someone in a formal way, we address the person with a special title of respect, along with a third person verb. Keep this concept in mind as we begin to learn about formal speech in German. Soon you will learn a similar construction in German that you can use to address people in a respectful, formal way.

LESSON 137

FORMAL SPEECH IN GERMAN

In the last lesson, we talked about informal speech and formal speech. We observed that with our family and friends, we speak to them with ordinary second person pronouns such as the word *you*. But with someone of high social rank we might speak to them in the third person—addressing them with a special title of respect, along with a third person verb.

The reason we told you all of that is because in German there is a similar way of speaking formally that involves speaking in the third person. Here's how it works: In German, if you want to address a friend, family member, or someone else you know, you would say **du** if speaking to only one person, or **ihr** if speaking to more than one person. But if you want to address someone you don't know very well, someone older than you, or someone important, you would instead use the following special title of respect: **Sie**. Note that the formal word **Sie** is always capitalized.

Now you may be saying to yourself, "Hey, wait a minute—that's confusing because the word **sie** already means *she* and *they*." And you are correct—it is somewhat confusing. The formal title **Sie** is a special formal pronoun that is third person plural. And, as a third person plural pronoun, it needs a third person plural verb to go along with it.

We have provided a chart to help you understand how **Sie** fits in with the other verbs and pronouns you know.

	SINGULAR	PLURAL
FIRST PERSON	**ich**	**wir**
SECOND PERSON	**du**	**ihr**
THIRD PERSON	**er/sie/es**	**sie** **Sie**

Notice that even though **Sie** is third person, we use it to address people as though it were second person. Also (and this is important, so pay attention), **Sie** can be used as both singular and plural—to speak to just one person or more than one person. Yes, you read that correctly—**Sie** is what you would use to speak formally to one person or more than one person—so **Sie** can be a formal way to say *you* and a formal way to say *y'all*.

EXAMPLES

Now that you get the basic idea of how formal speech works in German, let's work through some examples in which we use **Sie** (*you* or *y'all* addressing someone formally) and **sie** (*she* or *they*). Remember: to speak formally to someone, you will use the title **Sie** and a third person plural verb (but you will be using it to speak in the second person, addressing one or more people).

Here's our first example. It's simple, right?

> **Sie sind**.

This example, without further context, could be translated into English three different ways.

- *They are* (plural, could be informal or formal)
- *You are* (formal, singular)
- *Y'all are* (formal, plural)

The thing about this example that is confusing is the fact that the word **sie/Sie** comes first in the sentence. Any word that comes at the beginning of a sentence is going to be capitalized—so when we see that in writing, how do we know if the first word is the **sie** you already have been working with, or formal **Sie**? We don't. So this short sentence could be **sie sind**, just saying *they are*. Or, it could be a person speaking formally to just one person, saying **Sie sind,** which in that context would be a formal way to say *you are* to just one person. Or, since **Sie sind** can be both singular and plural, it could be a person speaking formally to more than one person, saying *y'all are* in a formal way.

Here's another example:

> **Sind Sie?**

This example is simpler than the previous one. It's a question, and since the word

Sie is not first in the sentence, we can see clearly that it is capitalized—so it really is the word **Sie**, not just regular **sie** with a capital *s* because it's the first word of a sentence. Therefore, this example could mean only two things, both formal speech. It could be a person speaking formally to one person, saying *Are you?* Or, it could be a person speaking formally to more than one person, saying *Are y'all?* Remember that grammatically speaking, **Sie sind** is third person plural, but we use it in formal speech both as a second person singular and a second person plural, so it does double-duty.

Here's another example:

Sie ist meine Schwester.

This example does not contain formal speech. Instead, the word at the beginning is just regular **sie** which can mean *she* or *they* (here it means *she*). The only reason that **sie** is capitalized is because it's the first word of the sentence.

The big clue here, though, is the verb: when you see the verb **ist** with **sie**, you know that it must mean *she.* You will never see formal **Sie** with **ist** as its verb, because **ist** is singular and formal **Sie** always takes a plural verb. So in a sentence like the one above, you can tell by looking at the verb that it isn't formal speech.

This might be a good time to mention pronouns—in certain situations, the pronouns **er** and **sie** can be translated into English as the neuter pronoun *it*, like in this short dialogue (the word **wo** in German means *where*):

- **Wo ist die Zeitung?** *(Where is the newspaper?)*
- **Sie ist auf dem Tisch.** *(It is on the table.)*

On the first line of that dialogue was the feminine noun **Zeitung**. Therefore, on the second line, when someone refers back to that feminine noun, the speaker must use the feminine pronoun **sie** for that purpose. You see, **Zeitung** is the antecedent of the pronoun **sie**, and the pronoun must agree in gender with its antecedent. So in this particular case, **sie** translates into English as *it.*

Here is one last example for this lesson:

Frau Smith und Herr Smith, haben Sie Kinder?

This example can only be interpreted one way—there is no confusion at all about its meaning. Since **Sie** is capitalized, you know it has to be formal speech. And since the speaker is addressing both Mrs. Schmidt and Mr. Schmidt at the same time, we know that **sind** and **Sie** are plural, meaning *y'all are*, but in a formal way. Therefore in this sentence the grammatically third person plural expression **haben Sie?** is being used to speak formally in the second person plural. So it can only be one thing: a formal way to say *Mrs. Smith and Mr. Smith, do y'all have children?*

So, this has been a long, tough lesson. But if you are learning German, it's very important that you learn how to use formal speech properly. In the exercises for this lesson, let's get some practice with formal speech so you can get the feeling of using the formal title **Sie** with third person verbs.

EXERCISES

1. **Sie sind.**
2. **Sie sind Herr Johnson.**
3. **Sind Sie Frau Smith?**
4. **Haben Sie einen Hund?**
5. **Haben sie einen Hund?**
6. **Haben Sie einen Hund, Frau Jones?**
7. **Hat sie einen Hund?**
8. **Wo ist die Zeitung?**
9. **Die Zeitung? Sie ist auf dem Stuhl.**
10. **Gehen Sie oft in den Supermarkt?**

Answers on page 204.

LESSON 138

FORMAL SPEECH AND POSSESSIVE ADJECTIVES

In German, when you use formal speech, you use a third person pronoun and a third person verb to speak to someone, like this:

Frau Jones, haben Sie Geld? *(Mrs./Miss/Ms. Jones, do you have money?)*

In other words, *you are using third person words as second person words.* But this method of using third person words as second person words doesn't just involve pronouns and verbs—it also extends to possessive adjectives.

The main point we want to make in this lesson pertains to the possessive adjective **ihr**. As you already know, **ihr** can mean *her* or *their*, like in this example:

Wir haben ihr Auto.

In that example, **ihr** could mean either *her* or *their*—so the sentence could read *We have her car* or it could say *We have their car.*

In this lesson, we are concerned with the word **ihr** when it means *their*. When **ihr** means *their*, it is a third person plural possessive adjective. And here's the important part: **ihr** is the possessive adjective you will use to say *your* or *y'all's* in formal speech.

Remember, the idea in formal speech is that you are using third person plural words as if they were second person words. So the third person word for *their* becomes the second person word *your* or *y'all's* when speaking formally to someone. Fortunately, we have one big thing that makes it easier to work with—when **ihr** is used formally, it's always capitalized, like this: **Ihr**.

Here's a chart that shows the various forms of the formal word **Ihr**:

	MASCULINE	FEMININE	NEUTER	PLURAL
NOMINATIVE (SUBJ./PRED. NOM.)	**Ihr**	**Ihre**	**Ihr**	**Ihre**
ACCUSATIVE (DIRECT OBJECT)	**Ihren**	**Ihre**	**Ihr**	**Ihre**
DATIVE (INDIRECT OBJECT)	**Ihrem**	**Ihrer**	**Ihrem**	**Ihren**

Again, notice that all these forms are capitalized.

Let's look at some examples with **Ihr**. Here's one to start with.

Herr Jones, haben Sie Ihr Geld?

In this sentence, the speaker is speaking formally to Mr. Jones. The speaker wants to say, *Mr. Jones, do you have your money?* But when the speaker gets to the part about *your money* he doesn't say **dein Geld**. That would be informal speech—the kind of speech you might use with friends or family. Instead, the speaker speaks formally, using the third person possessive adjective **Ihr**. So, speaking in this formal kind of way, the sentence reads *Mr. Jones, do you have your money?*

Now look carefully at this next example. What do you think it means?

Herr Jones, haben Sie ihr Geld?

In that example, notice that the word **ihr** was not capitalized. That means that the word **ihr** cannot possibly be formal speech. So this means that **ihr** must mean either *her* or *their*. So with that being the case, the sentence must read either as *Mr. Jones, do you have her money*, or *Mr. Jones, do you have their money?* So when you are reading German, you must look carefully to see what is capitalized and what isn't!

Here's another sneaky example—look very carefully!

Herr Jones, haben sie Ihr Geld?

In that example, **sie** is not capitalized, but **Ihr** is capitalized. Therefore **sie** can't be formal speech—but **Ihr** is definitely formal speech. What is going on?

Well, the word **sie** can't be referring to Mr. Jones. Uncapitalized **sie** can mean *she* or *they*. But in this particular case, since the verb is **haben**, we know that **sie** means *they*. In order for **sie** to mean *she* in this sentence, the verb would have to be **hat**, not **haben**.

The capitalized **Ihr** could mean *your* in a formal sense, referring to Mr. Jones. So the sentence could read *Mr. Jones, do they have your money?* But capitalized **Ihr** could also be a formal way to say *y'all's*, so the sentence could also read *Mr. Jones, do they have y'all's money?*

Here's yet another example. Again, look carefully!

Herr Jones, haben sie ihr Geld?

In this example, neither **sie** nor **ihr** is capitalized, so neither of them can be formal speech. The lower case **sie** could mean either *she* or *they*—but since the verb is **haben**, we know that **sie** has to mean *they* in this example sentence. The uncapitalized word **ihr** could mean either *her* or *their*, depending on the context—we don't have enough context to know who the speaker of the sentence is referring to. Therefore the sentence could read *Mr. Jones, do they have her money?* or *Mr. Jones, do they have their money?*

EXERCISES

1. **Gehen Sie mit Ihrer Frau ins Einkaufszentrum?**
2. **Herr Smith, haben Sie Ihr Auto?**
3. **Frau und Herr Jones, kaufen Sie ein Geschenk für Ihre Kinder?**
4. **Herr Johnson, wollen Sie über Ihre Katzen sprechen?**
5. **Frau Smith, Sie gehen nie ohne Ihr Geld ins Einkaufszentrum.**
6. **Herr Underwood, sprechen Sie Deutsch mit Ihrem Bruder?**
7. **Frau und Herr Smith, gehen Ihre Eltern jeden Tag in den Park?**
8. **Frau Johnson, ich gehe jede Woche mit Ihrer Schwester ins Kino.**
9. **Frau Underwood, brauchen Sie Essen?**
10. **Herr Smith, können Sie mir helfen? Wo ist mein Bruder?**

Answers on page 205.

LESSON 139

POSSESSION

Possessive words show ownership of something. In English, we often show possession by using an apostrophe followed by the letter *s*. Observe the following examples:

- <u>Fred's</u> car
- The <u>nation's</u> flag
- <u>Arizona's</u> capital

Sometimes we show possession by using the word *of*.

- The peak <u>of the mountain</u>
- The smell <u>of garlic</u>
- The beginning <u>of the show</u>

Therefore, in English, when you want to show possession of something, you must decide whether to use an apostrophe or the word *of*.

Here are a few of the most basic rules to remember when using apostrophes:

	RULE	EXAMPLE
RULE #1	To make a singular noun that **does not** end in *s* possessive, just add an apostrophe and an *s*.	Lauren always wants to borrow Kate's German book.
RULE #2	To make a singular noun that **does** end in *s* possessive, just add an apostrophe and an *s*.	The class's favorite subject was German.
RULE #3	To make a plural noun that ends in *s* possessive, add an apostrophe to the end of the word.	Due to increased interest in German, all the books' covers are starting to wear out.

LESSON 140

THE GENITIVE CASE

In German there are four noun cases. So far, you know three of the four: the nominative case, accusative case, and dative case. And now, it is time for you to learn the one remaining case, which is called the *genitive case*.

The genitive case is used to show possession. Using the genitive case, we can say things in German like *The man's cat* or *The girl's gift*. Let's start learning about the specifics of the genitive case in German by observing the genitive forms of the definite article. In this lesson, for the sake of simplicity, we are only going to teach you the feminine and plural forms of the genitive definite article. Here they are:

	MASCULINE	FEMININE	NEUTER	PLURAL
NOMINATIVE (SUBJ./PRED. NOM.)	der	die	das	die
ACCUSATIVE (DIRECT OBJECT)	den	die	das	die
DATIVE (INDIRECT OBJECT)	dem	der	dem	den
GENITIVE (POSSESSION)		der		der

As you may have noticed, these genitive forms look like forms from other cases. The feminine and plural forms of the genitive are **der**, which is the same as the nominative masculine form and the dative feminine form (we have circled these forms and connected them with a dotted line so you see the connections). This means that when you are reading, you'll have to pay attention to the context whenever you see the word **der** so you'll be able to determine what case it is.

In order to use the genitive case, we will take a noun and pair it with the appropriate form of the definite article. So if you want to say *of the woman*, you would take the word **Frau** and pair it with the feminine form of the genitive definite article, like this:

Der Frau

When you see a genitive form like the one above, it is important that you get the "feeling" of the genitive—that by its very nature it shows possession. Sort of like when are reading English and you see the word *woman's*. Just by looking at it, you get the feeling that it's possessing something. And you need to learn to get that same feeling from the genitive case in German.

In English, as we covered in the previous lesson, we can show possession either by using an apostrophe and the letter *s*, or by using the word *of*, like this:

- the <u>store's</u> manager
- the manager <u>of the store</u>

Whether we use an apostrophe and the letter *s*, or the word *of*, we know that the store somehow is possessing the manager, and that the manager somehow belongs to the store. As a native English speaker, when you see that apostrophe along with that letter *s*, it's a visual cue that it's showing possession, and without thinking too much about it, you get the feeling that it's possessing something.

In the same manner, when you are learning German, you need to get accustomed to the fact that the genitive case indicates possession in the same way that an apostrophe and *s* would in English. When you see the genitive case, you need to get the "feeling" that it is possessing something. If it helps you, you can imagine that the genitive case always includes the word *of*, as though the word *of* is somehow embedded in the genitive. In this way, train your mind to grasp the possessive meaning of the genitive case.

Let's study a few examples of the genitive case. Again, in this lesson, we are not learning the masculine or neuter forms of the genitive definite article—instead, we are covering just the feminine and plural forms. Here's your first example:

der Hund der Frau *(the dog of the woman* OR *the woman's dog)*

In that example, **der Frau** was genitive and feminine, so you know that the woman is possessing the dog. Here's another:

das Futter der Katze *(the food of the cat* OR *the cat's food)*

Again, in this example, **der Katze** is genitive, so you know that the cat is possessing the pet food. Here's an example with a plural genitive:

die Söhne der Männer *(the sons of the men OR the men's sons)*

In this example, the sons are belonging not to just one man, but to more than one man. Therefore **der Männer** is genitive and plural. Here's one last example:

die Katzen der Frauen *(the cats of the women OR the women's cats)*

Again, in this example, the cats belong not just to one woman, but to more than one woman—so **der Frauen** is both genitive and plural.

LESSON 141

THE GENITIVE CASE IN CONTEXT

In the last lesson, we started looking at some of the specifics of the genitive case. We learned how to use the feminine genitive definite article and the plural genitive definite article (we haven't looked at the masculine or neuter forms yet, though).

You may be confused by the fact that the article **der** can be nominative masculine, dative feminine, genitive feminine, or genitive plural. So when you see the word **der**, how on earth will you know what case it is? Here are some ways that you can use context to help yourself figure out what the word **der** is doing in a sentence when you see it.

First, a note about word order. When a noun in the genitive case is possessing another noun, there is a certain word order that it will follow. First will be the noun being possessed, then, right after that will be the noun in the genitive case which is possessing it. Here's an example:

das Auto der Frau *(the car of the woman OR the woman's car)*

In that example the woman is possessing the car. Notice that the car came first, then immediately after that, **der Frau** was in the genitive case. So, with that in mind, if you see **der** before a feminine noun and there is a noun directly before it, it's probably genitive. But if no noun precedes it, then **der** is probably not genitive, but instead dative feminine, like in this example:

Ich kaufe der Frau ein Auto. *(I'm buying the woman a car.)*

In that example, there was no noun directly before **der Frau**. Instead, **der Frau** is the indirect object, that is, the party that is benefiting or receiving in the sentence, so it's in the dative case. If you see **der Frau**, but there is no noun right before it, it very well could be dative. So in this way, word order can provide some good context to help you understand what is going on.

Here's another good contextual clue to help you: considering the gender of the noun that **der** goes with. You know that **der** can be nominative masculine, dative feminine, genitive feminine, or genitive plural. That's four choices! But considering the gender of the noun that **der** goes with can help you narrow it down. Take this for example:

der Mann

In that example, you know that **Mann** is masculine singular, so the definite article **der** can't possibly be dative or genitive. In order for **der** to be dative or genitive, the noun it goes with would have to be feminine or plural. So by taking note of the gender of the word **Mann**, you have narrowed down the possibilities for what **der** is doing in the sentence. You know that since **Mann** is masculine singular, the article **der** must be nominative.

der Frau

In that example, you know that **Frau** is feminine, so **der** cannot possibly be nominative. Whenever **der** is nominative, it has to be with a masculine noun, not a feminine one. So here, with **der** accompanying a feminine noun, it narrows the possibilities down to either dative or genitive. Therefore, **der Frau** could be the indirect object in a sentence, or it could be possessing something.

To review, here are the ways you can use context to help yourself translate and understand what is going on:

1. Observe the word order
2. Note the gender of the noun that the article is introducing

In the next lesson we will teach you the masculine and neuter forms of the definite article in the genitive case. In the meantime, translate these simple exercises.

EXERCISES

1. **Ich mag das Auto der Frau.**
2. **Die Hunde der Frauen sind im Park.**
3. **Wir wollen ein Geschenk für den Vater der Frau kaufen, aber wir haben kein Geld.**
4. **Siehst du den Hund der Frau jede Woche?**
5. **Mein Sohn spricht mit der Tochter der Frau.**
6. **Wir mögen die Autos der Männer.**
7. **Mein Bruder will das Auto der Frau kaufen, aber er hat kein Geld.**
8. **Ich mag die Schwester der Frau, aber ich mag den Bruder der Frau nicht.**
9. **Wo ist das Futter? Haben Sie das Futter der Katze?**
10. **Ihr habt das Geld der Männer nicht.**

Answers on page 205.

LESSON 142

MASCULINE AND NEUTER GENITIVE DEFINITE ARTICLES

PRONUNCIATION TIP: The *s* in **des** is a hissing *s* sound, not a *z* sound, so **des** sounds like *dess*.

A couple of lessons ago, we introduced you to the genitive case, and we started working with the genitive definite article in its feminine and plural forms. Now it is time to learn the genitive definite article in its masculine and neuter forms. Observe the genitive masculine and neuter definite articles in the chart below:

	MASCULINE	FEMININE	NEUTER	PLURAL
NOMINATIVE (SUBJ./PRED. NOM.)	der	die	das	die
ACCUSATIVE (DIRECT OBJECT)	den	die	das	die
DATIVE (INDIRECT OBJECT)	dem	der	dem	den
GENITIVE (POSSESSION)	des	der	des	der

Notice that the genitive masculine and genitive neuter definite articles are the same: **des**. Fortunately, these forms don't look like forms from any other cases, so they shouldn't be very confusing for you.

A few lessons ago, we learned that in addition to the definite article changing, nouns can change their spelling too. We noted that sometimes we have to add the letter *n* to the end of the dative plural form of a noun. And with the genitive case, we are going to change the ending, too (but not with the letter *n*).

Here's how it works: in the genitive case, masculine and neuter nouns get a new ending added—either *-es* or *-s*. But as we saw in the last couple of lessons, feminine and plural nouns do not get a new ending. The ending that you add to a genitive masculine or genitive neuter noun depends on how many syllables the word has. So read on, and we will see how these endings are applied to one-syllable words and multisyllable words.

178

ONE-SYLLABLE WORDS

For a genitive masculine noun that has just one syllable, first supply the definite article **des**, and then add *-es* to the end of the noun, like this:

des Mannes

And the same thing goes for a genitive neuter noun:

des Buches

A less common alternate spelling for genitive masculine and neuter nouns is to add only the letter *s*, like this:

* **des Manns**
* **des Buchs**

Although both forms are grammatically correct, the first form that ends in *-es* is generally preferred.

Here's a complete chart of all the forms of **der Mann**. The genitive singular is circled.

	SINGULAR	PLURAL
NOMINATIVE (SUBJ./PRED. NOM.)	der Mann	die Männer
ACCUSATIVE (DIRECT OBJECT)	den Mann	die Männer
DATIVE (INDIRECT OBJECT)	dem Mann	den Männern
GENITIVE (POSSESSION)	des Mannes	der Männer

WORDS WITH MORE THAN ONE SYLLABLE

For the genitive forms of masculine and neuter nouns with more than one syllable, supply the article **des** and then add only an additional *-s*, like this:

des Vaters

Here's a complete chart of all the forms of **der Vater**. The genitive singular is circled.

	SINGULAR	PLURAL
NOMINATIVE (SUBJ./PRED. NOM.)	**der Vater**	**die Väter**
ACCUSATIVE (DIRECT OBJECT)	**den Vater**	**die Väter**
DATIVE (INDIRECT OBJECT)	**dem Vater**	**den Vätern**
GENITIVE (POSSESSION)	**des Vaters**	**der Väter**

And don't forget: these endings also apply to neuter nouns. Since the word **Mädchen** has two syllables, we can use it as an example:

	SINGULAR	PLURAL
NOMINATIVE (SUBJ./PRED. NOM.)	**das Mädchen**	**die Mädchen**
ACCUSATIVE (DIRECT OBJECT)	**das Mädchen**	**die Mädchen**
DATIVE (INDIRECT OBJECT)	**dem Mädchen**	**den Mädchen**
GENITIVE (POSSESSION)	**des Mädchens**	**der Mädchen**

So if you want to show that something belongs to a man, do the same thing we did with feminine and plural nouns—put the genitive right after the thing being possessed, like this:

> **die Katze des Mannes** *(the cat of the man* OR *the man's cat)*

The noun **Vater** has more than one syllable so the genitive singular form would be **des Vaters**, as seen in this example:

> **die Zeitung des Vaters** *(the newspaper of the father* OR *the father's newspaper)*

And for the neuter noun **Mädchen**, the genitive singular is **des Mädchens**:

> **der Bruder des Mädchens** *(the brother of the girl* OR *the girl's brother)*

But if a masculine or neuter noun with more than one syllable ends with an *s* or an *s* sound, you must add *-es*. This is because it would be awkward to pronounce it if you only added another *s* to a word that already has an *s* sound at the end. An example of this would be the neuter noun **Kompass**, which means *compass*.

des Kompass<u>es</u>

EXERCISES

1. **Das Buch des Mannes ist in der Bibliothek.**
2. **Wir haben den Hund des Mädchens.**
3. **Ich mag die Katze des Mannes.**
4. **Meine Tochter will den Hund der Frau.**
5. **Der Junge spricht mit der Tochter des Mannes.**
6. **Wir haben die Geschenke der Mädchen.**
7. **Wir haben das Geld des Supermarkts nicht.**
8. **Sie kauft das Handy des Mannes nicht.**
9. **Der Vater des Mädchens ist mein Bruder.**
10. **Der Sohn des Mannes will immer Bücher lesen.**

Answers on page 205.

LESSON 143

THE GENITIVE WITH NAMES AND TITLES

For the last several lessons, we have been studying the genitive case. So far, you have learned how to use the genitive case with nouns that have a definite article, like this:

der Hund des Mannes *(the dog of the man OR the man's dog)*

And that's great. But there is more to tell about the genitive case and how it is used in German. For example, what if something belongs to a person and you want to use that person's name? In other words, what if you want to say things like these examples:

- Fred's cat
- Barbara's son
- Mr. Smith's computer
- Mrs. Johnson's car
- Ms. Green's book

Let's start with first names: if you want to put someone's first name in the genitive case, just add an *s*, like these examples:

- **Fred ⟶ Freds**
- **Mary ⟶ Marys**
- **Barbara ⟶ Barbaras**
- **John ⟶ Johns**

It's very similar to English, because we also add an *s* in English. But in English we use an apostrophe, whereas in German we just use an *s* without an apostrophe.

Now that you have put the person's name in the genitive case, put the thing being possessed *after* the person's name, like this:

- **Freds Katze** *(Fred's cat)*

- **Barbaras Hund** (*Barbara's dog*)

If you are using the title **Frau** with someone's name, just add an *s* to her last name, like this:

Frau Johnsons Hund (*Mrs./Miss/Ms. Johnson's dog*)

It's a long story, but the word **Herr** is part of a certain class of nouns called *weak nouns* or *weak masculine nouns*. For this reason, the word **Herr** will have the letter *n* at the end in all cases except the nominative case. So, if you want to say that **Herr Smith** is possessing something, you will need to put an *n* at the end of the word **Herr** and an *s* a the end of the word **Smith**, like this:

Herrn Smiths Katze (*Mr. Smith's cat*)

If the person's last name already ends with an *s*, *z*, or *x*, just add an apostrophe, like this:

Frau Jones' Hund (*Mrs./Miss/Ms. Jones's dog*)

EXERCISES

1. **Arnolds Sohn geht selten ins Kino.**
2. **Ja, Frau Jones' Schwester geht nie in den Park.**
3. **Bobs Katze ist auf dem Stuhl.**
4. **Mein Bruder will Herrn Smiths Auto kaufen.**
5. **Frau Johnson, haben Sie Frau Smiths Bücher?**
6. **Er will über Herrn Johnsons Kinder sprechen.**
7. **Herrn Smiths Frau geht selten ohne ihre Freundinnen ins Einkaufszentrum.**
8. **Mögen Freds Söhne Autos?**
9. **Spricht Herrn Smiths Schwester Deutsch?**
10. **Willst du ein Geschenk für Herrn Johnsons Vater kaufen?**

Answers on page 205.

LESSON 144

EIN-WORDS AND THE GENITIVE CASE

If you are reading this, that means that you have been sticking with us through a lot of material about the genitive case. The good news is that we are almost done with the genitive case, but the bad news is that we need to show you one last thing.

So far, you know how to use the genitive case with the definite article and with people's names—but what you don't know yet is how to use the genitive case with **ein** words. So, in this lesson, we are going to study how to put **ein** words in the genitive case. In the chart below, which uses **mein** as an example, observe the genitive forms of **ein** words:

	MASCULINE	FEMININE	NEUTER	PLURAL
NOMINATIVE (SUBJ./PRED. NOM.)	**mein**	**meine**	**mein**	**meine**
ACCUSATIVE (DIRECT OBJECT)	**meinen**	**meine**	**mein**	**meine**
DATIVE (INDIRECT OBJECT)	**meinem**	**meiner**	**meinem**	**meinen**
GENITIVE (POSSESSION)	**meines**	**meiner**	**meines**	**meiner**

Notice that just as with the definite article, some of the genitive forms of **ein** words are duplicates of other forms. For example, the genitive masculine **ein** word is the same as the genitive neuter **ein** word. And like their counterparts in the definite article chart (**des**), they both end with -es.

Likewise, the genitive feminine **ein** word is the same as the genitive plural **ein** word. And, like their counterparts in the definite article chart (**der**), they both end with -er. The dative feminine form also shares this same spelling.

Here's a little trick to help you remember these genitive form, and at the same time remember that they have the same endings as the genitive definite article. Look at the masculine and neuter genitive forms—they end with -es. The definite article which corresponds to those words would be **des**, which also ends with -es.

So here's the trick: take the word **mein**, add the corresponding definite article and remove the letter *d*.

mein + des = meindes - d = meines

So as you can see, if we take the word **mein** and add the genitive definite article, which is **des**, we get the word **meindes**. Then, remove the letter *d* and you are left with **meines**, which is the corresponding form of the **ein** word.

This trick works with the genitive feminine and plural forms, too:

mein + der = meinder - d = meiner

So again, if you add the definite article form to **mein**, and take away the *d*, you get the genitive from of the **ein** word. This little trick works with all genitive and dative forms, but not with the nominative or accusative forms.

Now let's examine how to use a genitive **ein** word in a sentence. When a genitive **ein** word possesses something, it goes immediately after the thing it possesses, like in these examples:

- **die Katze meiner Mutter** (*the cat of my mother* OR *my mother's cat*)
- **der Hund deines Vaters** (*the dog of your father* OR *your father's dog*)
- **der Sohn eines Mannes** (*the son of a man* OR *a man's son*)
- **die Töchter einer Frau** (*the daughters of a woman* OR *a woman's daughters*)

EXERCISES

1. **Die Söhne meines Bruders sind im Park.**
2. **Die Katze unserer Eltern ist auf dem Tisch.**
3. **Das Geld meiner Schwester ist auf dem Tisch.**
4. **Das Buch meiner Mutter ist auf dem Tisch.**
5. **Die Zeitung deines Vaters ist auf dem Stuhl.**
6. **Er mag das Auto meines Bruders.**
7. **Sie kauft oft ein Geschenk für den Sohn meines Freundes.**
8. **Das Handy eurer Schwester ist nicht auf dem Tisch.**
9. **Die Tochter meines Bruders liest immer Bücher.**
10. **Er hat das Geld meines Bruders.**

Answers on page 205.

LESSON 145

THE ESZETT

There is a special German letter that we haven't shown you yet. It's called **Eszett** (pronounced *ess-TSETT*). Here's an extra-large **Eszett** so you can get a good look at it.

ß

As you can see, it looks like a funny-shaped capitalized B. The **Eszett** is a fairly common letter, and we didn't want to write a beginning German book without at least introducing you to it. In English, it's sometimes called a *sharp s*.

The story of how the **Eszett** came into being is kind of a long one—you see, German used to be written with a heavy blackletter script, like this:

> Wiſſet, daß ihr nicht mit ver-
> gänglichem Silber oder Golde er-
> löſet ſeyd von eurem eiteln Wan-
> del, nach väterlicher Weiſe; ſon-
> dern mit dem theuren Blute
> Chriſti.

In that script, certain letters were connected to each other. When two characters are joined together into one character, that's called a *ligature*, from the Latin verb *ligo* which means "to tie" or "to bind." And that's what the **Eszett** is—a combination of *s* and *z*. The name of the German letter *s* is **es**, and the name of the German letter *z* is **zett** (pronounced *tsett*). Put them together and you get **Eszett**. So, the word **Eszett** just means *s-z*. The purpose of this character was to represent a hissing *s* sound—and since two *s*'s in a row also make a hissing *s* sound, the **Eszett** came to represent that, too.

186

Another interesting thing to know is that the letter *s* used to be written like this:

ſ

It looks sort of like an *f* without the horizontal line, right? So in blackletter script, a double *s* could be represented these two ways:

ſſ   ß

And you can see both of these on the first line of the sample of blackletter script that we showed you above. Let's take a look at that first line again:

The first word on that line is the word **wisset**. You can see that the *ss* in that word is represented by two of the *f* character. Then, the very next word is the word **daß**, which spelled with an **Eszett**. In a more modern text, that word would be spelled **dass**.

At one time, the **Eszett** was used in many more German words than it is now. In 1996, German-speaking countries got together and had a conference at which they decided to reform German spelling. This spelling reform removed the **Eszett** from some words. For example, before the spelling reform, the German word for *nut* was spelled **Nuß**, but they changed it to **Nuss**. Goodbye **Eszett**!

But there are still some words spelled with **Eszett**, such as the German word for fun which is **Spaß** and the German word for foot which is **Fuß**. The reason these words got to keep their **Eszett** is because they have long vowels. After a short vowel, the **Eszett** was replaced with a double *s*.

In Switzerland and Lichtenstein, the **Eszett** has been completely replaced with **ss**. So, words that typically take an **Eszett**, such as **Spaß**, would be spelled with **ss** in those countries.

GENERAL ADVICE

Congratulations! You made it all the way to the end of the book!

In closing, the authors would like to offer a few thoughts which you may find helpful. This book was designed to cover the beginning stages of German grammar in the easiest way possible. But, there is still a lot you do not know. So, here are a few thoughts and suggestions to help you continue your study of German.

First, we recommend that you take a closer look at the German verb system. In this book, we have tried to help you build a good foundation of knowledge about German verbs, but there is much more to verbs than we could cover here. For example, you still need to learn about the various German verb tenses, such as the several past tenses and the future tense.

Also, in order to make memorization easier, we have only made use of a small number of words. So, you should constantly strive to increase your German vocabulary. One way to do that is to use German in real-life situations. It may be difficult for you to find opportunities to speak German, but fortunately, the internet has made it easier to get in contact with other people who share your interests. Check our website for some helpful links to get you started.

Lastly, we would like to encourage you to always be aware of your pronunciation so that you can cultivate the most authentic German pronunciation possible. One way to do this is to take advantage of the many videos on YouTube which explain and demonstrate German pronunciation. Look for links to some of our favorites on our website.

Please take a moment to reflect on all you have learned. You have come a long way from lesson 1, and you are now ready to go further in your German studies. We, the authors, sincerely hope that this book has been enjoyable and profitable for you. We also hope that the knowledge you have gained from this book will become the foundation of a lifetime of enjoyment of the German language.

ANSWER KEY

LESSON SEVEN

1. Man
2. The man

LESSON NINE

1. Woman
2. The woman
3. Man
4. The man

LESSON TWELVE

1. Girl
2. The girl
3. Woman
4. The woman
5. Man
6. The man

LESSON 13

1. Plural
2. Singular
3. Singular
4. Singular
5. Plural
6. Singular
7. Plural
8. Plural
9. Plural
10. Singular

LESSON 16

1. The man
2. The men
3. The woman
4. The women
5. The girl
6. The girls

LESSON 17

1. The boy
2. The boys
3. The man
4. The men
5. The woman
6. The women
7. The girl
8. The girls

LESSON 18

1. The boy and the girl
2. The girls and the boys
3. The woman and the man
4. The women and the men
5. The girl and the woman
6. The boy and the man
7. The women and the girls
8. The girl
9. The boys
10. The boy

LESSON 20

1. A man
2. A man and a boy
3. The women and a man
4. A boy and a man
5. The girls and the boy
6. The woman and a man
7. The men and the boys
8. The girl
9. The woman and a boy
10. The girls and a boy

LESSON 21

1. A woman
2. A woman and a man
3. The women and a man
4. The men
5. The girl and a boy
6. The girls and a woman
7. The boys and the woman
8. The men and a boy
9. A man and a woman
10. The girl and a woman

LESSON 22

1. The girl
2. A girl
3. A woman and a girl
4. The girls and the boys
5. The women and the man
6. A woman and a man
7. A girl and a boy
8. The man and the woman
9. The women and the men
10. The boy and a man

LESSON 24

1. The brother
2. The brothers
3. A brother
4. The woman and the man
5. The girl and a boy
6. A woman and a man
7. The boys and the women
8. The boy and the woman
9. The men and the girls
10. The man and the women

LESSON 25

1. A sister and a brother
2. The brother and the sister
3. The sisters and the brothers
4. The girl and the boy
5. A girl and a boy
6. The boys and the girls
7. The woman and the man
8. The men and the women
9. The women and the girls
10. The boys and the girl

LESSON 26

1. *The brothers and the* (male) *friends*
2. *The sisters and the* (male) *friend*
3. *A* (male) *friend*
4. *The* (male) *friend*
5. *The* (male) *friends*
6. *A brother and a sister*
7. *The woman and the men*
8. *The girl and the boys*
9. *A girl and a boy*
10. *The girls and a woman*

LESSON 27

1. *The* (female) *friend*
2. *The* (female) *friends*
3. *The* (male) *friend*
4. *The friends* (male or of mixed gender)
5. *The sisters and a brother*
6. *The brothers and the sister*
7. *The girl and a woman*
8. *The girls and the boys*
9. *The boy and a girl*
10. *The man and the women*

LESSON 28

1. *My brother and my sister*
2. *My sister and my brothers*
3. *My* (female) *friend*
4. *My* (female) *friends*
5. *My sister and a* (male) *friend*
6. *The girl and the boy*
7. *The friends* (male or of mixed gender)
8. *The women and a* (male) *friend*
9. *My brothers and my* (male) *friend*
10. *My sister and a woman*

LESSON 29

1. *The man*
2. *My husband*
3. *A woman*
4. *My wife*
5. *My* (female) *friend and my wife*
6. *My brothers and my husband*
7. *The brothers and my sisters*
8. *My* (female) *friends and a boy*
9. *My sisters and the girl*
10. *My wife and the boys*

LESSON 31

1. *My son*
2. *My sons*
3. *My* (male) *friend and my wife*
4. *My sister and my sons*
5. *My son and my* (female) *friend/girlfriend*
6. *My husband and my sister*
7. *The* (male) *friend and the boy*
8. *My brother, my sons, and my* (female) *friend/girlfriend*
9. *My son and a girl*
10. *My* (female) *friends and a woman*

LESSON 32

1. *My daughter*
2. *My daughters*
3. *A son and a daughter*
4. *My sisters and my daughters*
5. *My husband and my brother*
6. *My* (female) *friend and my wife*
7. *The boys and the girl*
8. *The boy and the men*
9. *The woman and my* (male) *friend/boyfriend*
10. *A girl and a boy*

LESSON 34

1. *Your* (male) *friend/boyfriend*
2. *Your sister*
3. *Your* (female) *friends and my daughters*
4. *Your brothers and my sisters*
5. *Your* (female) *friend/girlfriend and my sister*
6. *A* (male) *friend and a* (female) *friend*
7. *Your daughter and my son*
8. *The boy and my* (female) *friend/girlfriend*
9. *The girl and the boys*
10. *The men and your sons*

LESSON 35

1. *The parents*
2. *My parents and your parents*
3. *Your sons and daughters*
4. *The women and my wife*
5. *My* (female) *friends*
6. *My friends* (male or of mixed gender)
7. *Your sister and your friends* (male or of mixed gender)
8. *My daughters and your brother*
9. *The girl and the boys*
10. *My husband and my sisters*

LESSON 36

1. *A child*
2. *My children*
3. *My daughter and your* (female) *friends*
4. *My parents and my husband*
5. *Your sisters and the children*
6. *My son and the boys*
7. *The child and the woman*
8. *Your wife and your sisters*
9. *A man and a woman*
10. *My daughters and my brothers*

LESSON 37

1. *Good day, my* (male) *friend.*
2. *See you later, my son.*
3. *Good evening, my friends* (male or of mixed gender).
4. *My daughter and your sister.*
5. *The man and my brothers.*
6. *My parents and your parents.*
7. *Your sons and the children.*
8. *The woman and the child.*
9. *A boy and a girl.*
10. *Your wife and your* (female) *friends.*

LESSON 38

1. *My father and my mother.*
2. *Your mother and your father.*
3. *The fathers and the mothers.*
4. *Good day, children.*
5. *See you later, Mother.*
6. *The men and the boys.*
7. *My sisters, my daughter, and my parents.*
8. *Your mother and a* (female) *friend.*
9. *The man and your brothers.*
10. *The child and my sons.*

LESSON 39

1. Kate (subject) walks (verb)
2. car (subject) is (verb)
3. sister (subject) likes (verb)
4. horse (subject) is (verb)
5. Harry (subject) told (verb)
6. Bob (subject) plays (verb)
7. Mark (subject) plays (verb)
8. brother (subject) cleans (verb)
9. Julia (subject) loves (verb)
10. students (subject) finished (verb)

LESSON 40

1. he (takes the place of *Alfred*)
2. it (takes the place of *locker room*)
3. she
4. they (takes the place of *kids*)
5. he (takes the place of *Johnny*)
6. we
7. they
8. you
9. it (takes the place of *rabbit*)
10. they (takes the place of *children*)

LESSON 41

1. *I am a child.*
2. *I am your brother.*
3. *I am your mother.*
4. *I am a man.*
5. *I am your husband.*
6. *The children and the parents.*
7. *Good day, mothers and fathers.*
8. *My children, my wife, and my parents.*
9. *My father and my son.*
10. *A girl and a boy.*

LESSON 42

1. *I am.*
2. *I am not your child!*
3. *I am not your brother.*
4. *See you later, my* (female) *friend.*
5. *I am not your mother.*
6. *My father and my wife.*
7. *Good day, my children.*
8. *My parents and my daughter.*
9. *My child and the girls.*
10. *Good evening, Mother and Father.*

LESSON 43

1. *You are my* (female) *friend/girlfriend.*
2. *You are not my brother.*
3. *I am your sister.*
4. *I am your mother.*
5. *Good day, my sons.*
6. *I am your daughter. I am not your son.*
7. *My father and your brother.*
8. *My parents and my friends* (male or of mixed gender).
9. *A woman and my sisters.*
10. *My daughters, my son, the men and the children.*

LESSON 44

1. *The man is my father.*
2. *The woman is my mother.*
3. *My sister is not your* (female) *friend/girlfriend.*
4. *My son is your* (male) *friend/boyfriend.*
5. *The child is not my brother.*
6. *You are my* (female) *friend/girlfriend.*
7. *Good day, fathers and mothers.*
8. *Your wife is my sister.*
9. *My* (female) *friends and your parents.*
10. *I am a boy.*

LESSON 45

1. *He is my father.*
2. *He is not my brother.*
3. *He is my child.*
4. *Anette is my mother and Fritz is my father.*
5. *You are not my brother.*
6. *I am your father.*
7. *My parents, your wife, and the children.*
8. *Your brother and a* (female) *friend.*
9. *My sister and a woman.*
10. *See you later, my* (male) *friend.*

LESSON 46

1. *She is my sister.*
2. *She is my mother.*
3. *She is not my daughter.*
4. *She is my* (female) *friend/girlfriend.*
5. *See you later, Mother.*
6. *He is my* (male) *friend/boyfriend.*
7. *He is not my child.*
8. *I am your brother.*
9. *You are my father.*
10. *The girl is not my daughter.*

LESSON 47

1. *It is evening.*
2. *It is night.*
3. *It is day.*
4. *It is morning.*
5. *She is a woman.*
6. *He is not my brother.*
7. *He is a man.*
8. *Good evening, my* (male) *friend!*
9. *Good day, Father!*
10. *He is my son.*

LESSON 48

1. **nicht**
2. **kein**
3. **kein**
4. **nicht**
5. **kein**
6. **nicht**
7. **nicht**
8. **kein**
9. **kein**
10. **nicht**

LESSON 49

1. *She is not a mother (she is no mother).*
2. *He is not a boy (he is no boy).*
3. *It is evening.*
4. *He is a child.*
5. *You are not a* (male) *friend (you are no* (male) *friend).*
6. *I am not your son.*
7. *You are not my* (female) *friend/girlfriend.*
8. *He is not my husband.*
9. *The parents, a woman and a boy.*
10. *The girls and a woman.*

LESSON 50

1. *We are children.*
2. *We are your parents.*
3. *We are not friends.*
4. *You are my mother.*
5. *She is not my* (female) *friend/girlfriend.*
6. *The man is not my father.*
7. *Good evening, my daughter.*
8. *I am your husband.*
9. *My mother is my* (female) *friend.*
10. *My* (female) *friends and your children.*

LESSON 51

1. *Y'all are children.*
2. *Y'all are my parents.*
3. *Y'all are my friends* (male or of mixed gender).
4. *Good day, my* (male) *friend.*
5. *We are not your daughters.*
6. *She is my* (female) *friend/girlfriend.*
7. *It is morning.*
8. *You are not a boy.*
9. *He is my brother.*
10. *I am not your sister.*

LESSON 52

1. *My sons are your* (male) *friends.*
2. *The men are my brothers.*
3. *The women are my sisters and my wife.*
4. *Y'all are my parents.*
5. *The girls are my daughters.*
6. *We are your children.*
7. *He is my* (male) *friend/boyfriend.*
8. *She is my wife.*
9. *It is night.*
10. *You are my mother.*

LESSON 53

1. *They are my sisters.*
2. *They are my* (female) *friends.*
3. *They are not my daughters.*
4. *Y'all are my sisters.*
5. *We are your friends and brothers.*
6. *She is my mother.*
7. *You are not a boy. You are a man.*
8. *I am not a father.*
9. *You are not my son. You are my daughter.*
10. *We are not your children. We are your parents.*

LESSON 54

1. *Good day, Mr. Smith.*
2. *See you later, Mrs./Miss/Ms. Smith.*
3. *Hans is my husband.*
4. *Mrs./Miss/Ms. Jones is not my sister.*
5. *They are my parents and your children.*
6. *Y'all are my friends* (male or of mixed gender).
7. *He is my father and she is my mother.*
8. *It is day.*
9. *We are not fathers.*
10. *You are a girl and I am a woman.*

LESSON 55

1. I (first person singular)
2. you (second person singular)
3. she (third person singular)
4. we (first person plural)
5. y'all (second person plural)
6. they (third person plural)
7. he (third person singular)
8. it (third person singular)
9. y'all (second person plural)
10. flowers (third person plural)

LESSON 57

1. *You are not my dog. You are my cat.*
2. *The cat is my friend.*
3. *We are not dogs. We are cats.*
4. *Mr. Smith is not my father. He is my brother.*
5. *Y'all are my dogs.*
6. *Your mother is my sister.*
7. *We are not your friends. We are your parents.*
8. *Sarah is your sister. She is my* (female) *friend/girlfriend.*
9. *Mr. and Mrs. Jones are my parents.*
10. *She is my sister and he is my brother.*

LESSON 58

1. *A man.* OR *One man.*
2. *Two women, three children, four cats, and five dogs.*
3. *356-0142 (three five six zero one four two).*
4. *Two boys and five women.*
5. *Six dogs and four cats.*
6. *They are my daughters.*
7. *We are not your parents.*
8. *Y'all are my brothers.*
9. *Mr. Smith is my father. Helga is my sister.*
10. *You are not a child.*

LESSON 59

1. *Seven friends* (male or of mixed gender).
2. *Nine boys and twelve girls.*
3. *790-8415 (seven nine zero eight four one five).*
4. *Ten dogs and twelve cats.*
5. *The woman is my* (female) *friend/girlfriend. Arnold is my brother.*
6. *I am your sister and you are my brother.*
7. *She is not your* (female) *friend/girlfriend.*
8. *Mrs. Smith is not my sister. She is my mother.*
9. *They are not my children.*
10. *We are the parents and y'all are the children.*

LESSON 60

1. *The chair.*
2. *Nine children and eight chairs!*
3. *Eleven cats and seven dogs.*
4. *Two sisters and six brothers.*
5. *Five cats and three dogs.*
6. *We are not dogs. We are cats.*
7. *Mr. Jones is not my brother. He is my son.*
8. *You are my* (male) *friend/boyfriend.*
9. *The men are my brothers.*
10. *Good day, Jürgen.*

LESSON 61

1. *Eleven tables and eight chairs.*
2. *Five chairs and seven tables.*
3. *A cat and nine dogs.*
4. *The table and a chair.*
5. *Good day, Sarah.*
6. *Y'all are cats. Y'all are not dogs.*
7. *It is not a table. It is a chair.*
8. *She is my sister. He is my brother.*
9. *The man and the woman are my parents.*
10. *The boys are my sons.*

LESSON 62

1. newspaper
2. movie
3. trombone
4. baseball
5. fish
6. radio
7. building
8. speech
9. wallet
10. deer

LESSON 63

1. predicate nominative
2. direct object
3. direct object
4. direct object
5. direct object
6. predicate nominative
7. direct object
8. direct object
9. predicate nominative
10. direct object

LESSON 64

1. **den** (direct object)
2. **der** (predicate nominative)
3. **der** (subject)
4. **den** (direct object)
5. **der** (predicate nominative)
6. **den** (direct object)
7. **der** (predicate nominative)
8. **der** (subject)
9. **den** (direct object)
10. **der** (predicate nominative)

LESSON 65

1. **einen** (direct object)
2. **mein** (predicate nominative)
3. **dein** (subject)
4. **mein** (predicate nominative)
5. **keinen** (direct object)
6. **einen** (direct object)
7. **kein** (predicate nominative)
8. **ein** (subject)
9. **deinen** (direct object)
10. **meinen** (direct object)

LESSON 66

1. *I have the dog.*
2. *I have a daughter.*
3. *I have the chair.*
4. *I do not have a chair.*
5. *I do not have a husband.*
6. *They are my friends* (male or of mixed gender).
7. *I have a son and a daughter.*
8. *I am your mother.*
9. *Y'all are my* (female) *friends.*
10. *I have a dog.*

LESSON 67

1. *I have a wife.*
2. *I do not have a daughter.*
3. *I do not have the chair.*
4. *I do not have your dog.*
5. *I have a cat.*
6. *You are not my* (male) *friend/boyfriend.*
7. *Y'all are my parents.*
8. *I am your father.*
9. *I do not have daughters.*
10. *I have a cat.*

LESSON 68

1. *I have a car.*
2. *I do not have your car.*
3. *I have two children, three cats, and a dog.*
4. *I have seven sisters and eight brothers.*
5. *You are my daughter. I am your father.*
6. *I do not have a chair.*
7. *We are brothers and sisters.*
8. *I have your dog.*
9. *Y'all are my friends.*
10. *I have a cat and a dog.*

LESSON 69

1. *You have a car and I have two cars.*
2. *You have a table.*
3. *I have the dog. I do not have the cat.*
4. *You have three sisters and five brothers.*
5. *You have ten cats and three dogs.*
6. *He is not my father. He is Mr. Johnson.*
7. *You are my* (female) *friend. We are* (female) *friends.*
8. *You do not have children.*
9. *It is a cat. It is not a dog!*
10. *You do not have a chair.*

LESSON 70

1. *She has a dog.*
2. *The child does not have a cat. He/She/It has a dog.*
3. *You have a table and two chairs.*
4. *My daughter has my car.*
5. *He has nine children—two sons and seven daughters.*
6. *I am your* (male) *friend/boyfriend.*
7. *You have ten sisters and a brother.*
8. *We are not your parents.*
9. *They are my friends and y'all are my brothers.*
10. *Arnold has the dog.*

LESSON 71

1. *I do not have a dog, but my mother has a dog.*
2. *You do not have a cat, but your* (male) *friend/boyfriend has a cat.*
3. *My cat is my friend and your dog is your friend.*
4. *My brother has my car.*
5. *I have four dogs and five cats.*
6. *Mrs./Miss/Ms. Smith has your dog.*
7. *Sonja is my* (female) *friend, but Peter is not my* (male) *friend.*
8. *You have six children, but I have nine children.*
9. *My son has a cat and a dog.*
10. *He has three chairs, but I have the table.*

LESSON 72

1. *We do not have a car, but you have five cars.*
2. *We do not have a brother, but we have three sisters.*
3. *We have a dog, but we do not have a cat.*
4. *My wife has the car.*
5. *I do not have your dog.*
6. *The girls are my sisters and the boys are my brothers.*
7. *She has a son and five daughters.*
8. *We do not have a son, but we have a daughter.*
9. *Mr. Jones does not have a wife, but he has eight sisters.*
10. *You are my sister, but you are not my* (female) *friend.*

LESSON 73

1. *Y'all have my car.*
2. *Y'all have my dog and my cat.*
3. *Y'all have eleven children, but we have no children.*
4. *The boy has my dog.*
5. *The girl does not have a dog.*
6. *You have no sisters, but I have twelve sisters and a brother.*
7. *My sister has the chair.*
8. *They are my children.*
9. *The children are your brothers and your sisters.*
10. *She is not my (female) friend/girlfriend. She is my wife.*

LESSON 74

1. *She has my car!*
2. *They do not have a dog, but we have six dogs.*
3. *Y'all do not have a dog.*
4. *I have four cats and eight dogs.*
5. *The boys are my sons and the girl is my daughter.*
6. *My brothers have my car.*
7. *Mr. Smith has six brothers, but I do not have a brother.*
8. *You have a dog and a cat.*
9. *My sister has a dog, but my mother has a cat.*
10. *We do not have a car, but you have five cars.*

LESSON 76

1. *We have a dog. Dieter and Nina have a dog too.*
2. *I have a son. My (female) friend/girlfriend Natascha also has a son.*
3. *She has eight cats and ten dogs.*
4. *My dog is my friend.*
5. *You have four daughters, but I have seven daughters.*
6. *Simon has a sister, but he does not have a brother.*
7. *She is my mother.*
8. *You have a mother and a father. They are your parents.*
9. *I am a woman and you are a man.*
10. *They have five cars, but y'all do not have a car.*

LESSON 79

1. *He has my money!*
2. *We have money—six euros and twelve dollars.*
3. *My father does not have money.*
4. *The boy has eight dollars.*
5. *My sisters have my money.*
6. *My brother has money, but I do not have money.*
7. *You do not have money, but I have five euros.*
8. *Y'all have ten dollars, but we do not have money.*
9. *They have money—five euros and two dollars.*
10. *Your brother does not have money, but your sister has ten dollars.*

LESSON 80

1. *My father has his dog.*
2. *My brother has his cats.*
3. *He has his money.*
4. *Mr. Jones has his car, but you do not have your car.*
5. *She has nine dollars, but I do not have money.*
6. *They have seven dollars and two euros.*
7. *I have ten euros, but my (female) friend/girlfriend does not have money.*
8. *We have a dog, but y'all have cats.*
9. *She has two cars, but she does not have money.*
10. *The children have the dog.*

LESSON 81

1. *My mother has her dog.*
2. *My sister has her cats.*
3. *She has her money, but y'all do not have money.*
4. *Mrs./Miss/Ms. Jones has a car. Her (female) friend also has a car.*
5. *My brother has a dog.*
6. *Her father has a car, but we do not have a car.*
7. *Her mother has seven cats and a dog.*
8. *The girl has a dog, but she does not have a cat.*
9. *Mr. Smith has four cats and a dog.*
10. *He has a car, but I do not have a car.*

LESSON 82

1. *The girl has her/his money.*
2. *The boys have her money.*
3. *The woman has her dog.*
4. *My sister has her dog, but she does not have her cat.*
5. *We do not have a car, but they have three cars.*
6. *I have a cat. My* (male) *friend/boyfriend also has a cat.*
7. *You do not have money, but your father has money.*
8. *Y'all are my sisters and they are my brothers.*
9. *My sister has seven dollars.*
10. *Her brother has two cars, but he does not have money.*

LESSON 83

1. *The dog has the newspaper!*
2. *My sister has her books and my father has his newspaper.*
3. *We have the books.*
4. *Mrs./Miss/Ms. Jones has money, but Mr. Smith does not have money.*
5. *My brother has a dog.*
6. *Her father has two daughters, but he does not have sons.*
7. *Her mother has seven cats.*
8. *Her brother has a dog, but he does not have a cat.*
9. *Y'all are my sisters, but they are my brothers.*
10. *My* (female) *friend/girlfriend has a car. I also have a car.*

LESSON 84

1. *They have our dog!*
2. *He has our newspaper.*
3. *Our father is his brother.*
4. *The dog has our book!*
5. *We have our books and my mother has her newspaper.*
6. *Y'all have our newspaper.*
7. *Your* (female) *friends have our car.*
8. *They have eight dollars, but we do not have money.*
9. *Mr. Smith has three dogs and a cat.*
10. *I am a cat, but you are a dog.*

LESSON 85

1. *I have y'all's chair.*
2. *Y'all's sister is my* (female) *friend/girlfriend.*
3. *We have y'all's car.*
4. *Y'all's dog has our newspaper.*
5. *He has y'all's books.*
6. *The girl has her/his books.*
7. *My sister has y'all's books.*
8. *We have her money.*
9. *Mrs./Miss/Ms. Smith has five dogs and two cats.*
10. *We are sisters and he is our brother.*

LESSON 86

1. *They have her/their table.*
2. *He has her/their books.*
3. *We have her/their car.*
4. *The dog has her/their newspaper!*
5. *We have her/their books.*
6. *Y'all's sister is my* (female) *friend/girlfriend.*
7. *They have y'all's dog.*
8. *She has her/their newspaper and I have our books.*
9. *The boy has his book.*
10. *They are my parents. They do not have money.*

LESSON 88

1. *Y'all are hungry.*
2. *He is not hungry.*
3. *His cat is thirsty.*
4. *Our dogs are thirsty.*
5. *You do not have her/their car.*
6. *Her/their daughter has a car, but my son does not have a car.*
7. *My dog is hungry, but my cat is not hungry.*
8. *We have y'all's books and also y'all's newspapers.*
9. *She has her/their money—two dollars and seven euros.*
10. *The children are our sons and daughters.*

LESSON 89

1. *The dog has our food.*
2. *We do not have food but my friends have food.*
3. *The cats have her/their food.*
4. *My children are hungry, but I do not have food.*
5. *Y'all's dog has food.*
6. *Your son is hungry, but he does not have money.*
7. *Y'all's sons have their/her books.*
8. *My mother has her/their money—nine dollars and five euros.*
9. *Y'all's cats are thirsty.*
10. *You are my* (male) *friend/boyfriend and he is my brother.*

LESSON 90

1. *I am thirsty, but I do not have water.*
2. *My cat is thirsty, but she does not have water.*
3. *Y'all's cats have food, but they do not have water.*
4. *The boy is thirsty, but he has no water.*
5. *My cat is hungry, but she does not have food.*
6. *My brother does not have money. His wife also does not have money.*
7. *Our children are hungry and thirsty.*
8. *Y'all's daughter has y'all's dog.*
9. *She is my mother and her sister is Mrs./Miss/Ms. Jones.*
10. *My father has his newspaper.*

LESSON 91

1. *Our dog needs food.*
2. *I need a newspaper and food.*
3. *We are thirsty. We need water.*
4. *His children need food, but they do not have money.*
5. *They need a cat.*
6. *The dog is hungry. He needs food.*
7. *You are not a cat. You are a dog.*
8. *Y'all's children need books.*
9. *Her/Their mother needs a dog.*
10. *My* (male) *friend/boyfriend has a car, but he does not need his car.*

LESSON 92

1. direct object: *money*
   indirect object: *friend*
2. direct object: *money*
   indirect object: *charity*
3. direct object: *example*
   indirect object: *class*
4. direct object: *curtains*
   indirect object: *house*
5. direct object: *seeds*
   indirect object: *garden*
6. direct object: *sandwiches*
   indirect object: *us*
7. direct object: *story*
   indirect object: *judge*
8. direct object: *song*
   indirect object: *audience*
9. direct object: *copies*
   indirect object: *everyone*
10. direct object: *shirt*
    indirect object: *me*

LESSON 95

1. *We are giving the child the money.*
2. *I am giving the man a car.*
3. *He is giving his daughter the car.*
4. *They are giving your child the books.*
5. *She is giving her husband the money.*
6. *You are giving y'all's daughter the newspaper.*
7. *Helga is giving her/their child the money.*
8. *Y'all are giving the dog food and water.*
9. *Our cat is thirsty and she needs water.*
10. *Y'all are sisters and we are brothers.*

LESSON 96

1. **Mädchen**
2. **Jungen**
3. **Brüdern**
4. **Schwestern**
5. **Freunden**
6. **Freundinnen**
7. **Söhnen**
8. **Töchtern**
9. **Kindern**
10. **Vätern**

LESSON 97

1. *I am giving the man the gift.*
2. *I am giving the men the gifts.*
3. *We are giving my sisters a gift.*
4. *Y'all need a gift.*
5. *My sisters are giving our parents the car.*
6. *You need food, but you do not have money.*
7. *We are giving the children our gift.*
8. *Her/Their dog needs water. His dog also needs water.*
9. *My* (female) *friend/girlfriend is giving her/their sister her dog.*
10. *The girl gives the dog its food.*

LESSON 98

1. *I am buying my mother a gift.*
2. *My sisters are buying our parents a gift.*
3. *Y'all are buying the cats food.*
4. *She is buying her/their son a car.*
5. *Y'all are buying y'all's parents a table.*
6. *We are buying his children a gift.*
7. *The boys need water.*
8. *The dogs are hungry and they need food.*
9. *You are giving my brother your newspaper.*
10. *Y'all are our* (female) *friends.*

LESSON 102

1. *I am giving my brother the phone.*
2. *Your sister has my phone.*
3. *My brother is giving his* (male) *friend his phone.*
4. *My mother has your phone.*
5. *I am buying my daughters a phone.*
6. *We have no phone, no car and no money.*
7. *My* (male) *friend/boyfriend has two phones. I also have two phones.*
8. *We are giving the children gifts.*
9. *The children are hungry, but they have no food.*
10. *We are buying my sons phones.*

LESSON 104

1. *I am helping my father.*
2. *I am helping the children.*
3. *You are helping her/their mother.*
4. *We are helping your father.*
5. *They are helping the dogs.*
6. *I am not helping your father.*
7. *We are buying our sons cars.*
8. *I do not have a phone, but my husband has a phone.*
9. *The girl has her book, but my sons do not have a book.*
10. *Y'all are giving my sisters money.*

LESSON 106

1. *I help his father every day.*
2. *I give my cats food every morning.*
3. *Y'all buy y'all's dogs food every week.*
4. *He helps his mother every week.*
5. *You give the children gifts every evening.*
6. *I give my wife my phone every day.*
7. *They are not helping the children.*
8. *Her/Their dogs need food every day.*
9. *We need food, but my husband has no money.*
10. *His friends* (male or of mixed gender)*are hungry, but we do not have any food.*

LESSON 107

1. *I help you every day.*
2. *My mother helps me every day.*
3. *We are buying you a car.*
4. *My mother is buying me a phone.*
5. *They are buying their/her son a car, but we have no money.*
6. *My dog is helping me.*
7. *Y'all give y'all's dogs and cats food every day.*
8. *We need a newspaper.*
9. *I am buying his mother a newspaper.*
10. *I give the children books every week.*

LESSON 108

1. *I speak German.*
2. *The children are giving their mothers a gift.*
3. *My sister speaks German every day, but my brothers speak English.*
4. *I speak German, but my daughters speak English.*
5. *Y'all's parents are giving gifts to the children.*
6. *My mother speaks German, but my sisters speak English.*
7. *My mother is buying me gifts.*
8. *We are helping the children.*
9. *My brother is buying his daughter a phone.*
10. *We need food, but we do not have any money.*

LESSON 109

1. *I read two books every week.*
2. *My sister reads three books every day!*
3. *The girl is reading her book.*
4. *They are not reading the books.*
5. *I am buying you a book.*
6. *You read books every day.*
7. *My daughter and her* (female) *friends read four books every week.*
8. *My brother does not speak German, but he speaks English.*
9. *They help me every week.*
10. *Y'all are giving the children phones.*

LESSON 110

1. *My father likes to read the newspaper every morning.*
2. *We do not like to give our brother money.*
3. *His parents like to give the children gifts.*
4. *You like to read books, but your brother does not like to read.*
5. *My brother likes to help me.*
6. *My sister likes to buy her* (female) *friends gifts.*

7. *I like to speak German, but my* (female) *friends like to speak English.*
8. *We are giving you the phone.*
9. *I do not like to buy newspapers.*
10. *My* (female) *friend/girlfriend is giving her son her car and my father is giving me his car.*

LESSON 111

1. *We always speak German, but Thomas and Marina never speak German.*
2. *My friends* (male or of mixed gender) *always have money, but they never give me money.*
3. *You buy your dog food every day.*
4. *Y'all are giving the children gifts.*
5. *I buy you food every week.*
6. *We are helping the children, but we do not give the children money.*
7. *Y'all are buying the mothers and fathers gifts.*
8. *My son likes to read books, but I never read books.*
9. *My dog does not have your book.*
10. *Their/Her children are hungry. My children are hungry too.*

LESSON 112

1. *I like your phone.*
2. *You like books, but I do not like to read.*
3. *My sisters do not like your car, but I like your car.*
4. *My children do not like cats—they like dogs.*
5. *I like to speak German, but my son always speaks English.*
6. *My sisters are buying you a gift.*
7. *We speak German every day.*
8. *My parents are buying me a car, but they do not have any money.*
9. *You are buying the dogs food, but they do not need food.*
10. *I always help my sisters, but my sisters never help me.*

LESSON 113

1. Preposition: *behind*
   Object of preposition: *couch*
2. Preposition: *beside*
   Object of preposition: *lamp*
3. Preposition: *in*
   Object of preposition: *trunk*
4. Preposition: *through*
   Object of preposition: *tunnel*
5. Preposition: *under*
   Object of preposition: *house*
6. Preposition: *before*
   Object of preposition: *lunch*
7. Preposition: *after*
   Object of preposition: *school*
8. Preposition: *by*
   Object of preposition: *post office*
9. Preposition: *on*
   Object of preposition: *campus*
10. Preposition: *beyond*
    Object of preposition: *mountain*

LESSON 114

1. *Mrs./Miss/Ms. Smith likes to read books with our children every week.*
2. *You like to speak German with me.*
3. *She speaks English with her brothers every day.*
4. *I speak German with you every week, but I do not like to speak German.*
5. *Y'all never speak English with me—y'all always speak German.*
6. *We like to read the newspaper every day.*
7. *My (male) friend/boyfriend is buying a phone.*
8. *The boy likes dogs, but he has a cat.*
9. *We like to read books with our friends (male or of mixed gender).*
10. *They never buy me books.*

LESSON 115

1. *I am buying a book about cats.*
2. *My brother has a book about cars, but he does not have a car.*
3. *We are talking about our dog—he does not have water.*
4. *We like to read the newspaper every day, but they never read the newspaper.*
5. *He is buying me a newspaper.*
6. *Y'all do not like to speak English, but we speak English every day.*
7. *We give the boys and girls money every week.*
8. *My brother has five dollars, but he does not like to give me money.*
9. *My friends* (male or of mixed gender) *like cars, but I like books.*
10. *We need a car, be we do not have any money.*

LESSON 116

1. *I am buying a car for my son.*
2. *Mrs. Johnson is buying a gift for her husband.*
3. *We do not have money, but we are buying phones for our children.*
4. *We like books and we always read books with our children.*
5. *Y'all speak English, but we speak German.*
6. *Mrs./Miss/Ms. Smith buys her dogs food every week.*
7. *Mrs./Miss/Ms. Smith buys food for her dogs every week.*
8. *The boy likes to read books about cats.*
9. *I never speak German with you.*
10. *You always give your father money.*

LESSON 117

1. *I am buying you a gift.*
2. *I am buying a gift for you.*
3. *You are buying me a gift.*
4. *You are buying a gift for me.*
5. *Your mother speaks German, but your father speaks English.*
6. *I like you, but you do not like me.*
7. *My daughter does not like cats.*
8. *The boys have a gift for you.*
9. *My dog likes his food.*
10. *My (male) friend/boyfriend does not like to give his daughter his phone.*

LESSON 118

1. *Do you like speaking English with your* (female) *friends?*
2. *Do you like me?*
3. *Does Mrs./Miss/Ms. Johnson have a dog?*
4. *Are you buying my son a gift?*
5. *Do y'all have a cat?*
6. *Is she your* (female) *friend/girlfriend?*
7. *Do you have food and water for your dog?*
8. *Does your daughter have a phone?*
9. *My parents are talking about the children.*
10. *My friends* (male or of mixed gender) *never buy me gifts.*

LESSON 119

1. *Do you buy food every day?*
2. *No, I buy food every week.*
3. *Does your brother have a child?*
4. *Yes, my brother has three daughters.*
5. *Do the men have a gift for me?*
6. *Yes, the men have a gift for you.*
7. *Are you a mother?*
8. *No, I am not a mother.*
9. *Do y'all like reading books with y'all's children?*
10. *Yes, we read books every day.*

LESSON 122

1. *I go to the cinema with my* (female) *friends every week.*
2. *Do your parents go to the supermarket every day?*
3. *No, they go to the supermarket every week.*
4. *My sister goes to school every week.*
5. *Are you buying me a gift?*
6. *I always go to school with my brother.*
7. *Y'all never read books about money.*
8. *We have a gift for you.*
9. *The girls are going to the supermarket, but they have no money.*
10. *They like to go to the cinema with their/her children.*

LESSON 123

1. *My brothers are going to the cinema with their friends* (male or of mixed gender) *now.*
2. *Is my son going to school today?*
3. *My sons are reading a book about dogs and cats today.*
4. *The boys are buying a gift for their/her dog.*
5. *My* (female) *friends are going to the supermarket with their children.*
6. *We are talking about our children.*
7. *I do not like Alex, but I like his car.*
8. *Do our daughters like to go to the cinema every week?*
9. *Yes, and they are going to the cinema with their friends* (female) *today.*
10. *The boys are buying me a gift.*

LESSON 125

1. *We go to the mall every week, but they never go to the mall.*
2. *Are the boys going to the mall today?*
3. *No, but they go to the mall with their parents every week.*
4. *Your father never goes to school, but your sister goes to school every day.*
5. *My wife is reading a book with our children.*
6. *We like cars and I am reading a book about cars today.*
7. *I speak with my sisters every day, but I do not speak with my brother every day.*
8. *Is your mother going to the supermarket with you today?*
9. *Are you buying a gift for me today?*
10. *Are you going to the mall with me today?*

LESSON 126

1. *Arnold is going to the park with his dogs today.*
2. *Are y'all going to the park with y'all's children today?*
3. *They never go to the park, but their sons go to the park every day with their dogs.*
4. *My son does not like reading books, but he goes to the library every day.*
5. *We always speak German, but my parents never speak German.*
6. *I am buying food for my dogs today.*
7. *They are buying the girl a gift.*
8. *Are y'all talking about our dog?*
9. *Yes, we are talking about y'all's dog.*
10. *I am helping you. Are you helping me?*

LESSON 127

1. *You often go to the park with your dog, but you seldom go to the park with me.*
2. *You do not often go to the supermarket, but I go to the supermarket every day.*
3. *I seldom go to the mall, but I go to the library every week.*
4. *Are y'all going to the cinema with y'all's friends* (male or of mixed gender) *now?*
5. *Do your sisters go to the mall with you often?*
6. *No, my sisters never go the the mall with me, but they go every day with their* (female) *friends.*
7. *My parents are buying you a gift, but they are not buying a gift for me.*
8. *We have your books and we are going to the library now.*
9. *Her/Their son is going to school today, but my son does not go to school today.*
10. *Our friends* (male or of mixed gender) *are going to the park today with their/her children and dogs, but they do not like the park.*

LESSON 128

1. *She never goes to the mall without her money.*
2. *We seldom go to the park, but our* (male) *friend Peter goes every day.*
3. *They never go to the library without their books.*
4. *Are you buying a gift for my dog?*
5. *You like to read books in the library every day.*
6. *Helga goes to the library every week.*
7. *I am buying my father a book, but he never buys me gifts.*
8. *Your sister likes books, but she never goes to the library.*
9. *The girl likes helping her father, but she never helps you.*
10. *Are we going to the supermarket today?*

LESSON 129

1. *We are often in/at the school.*
2. *They are in/at the park with their/her friends.*
3. *Are y'all in/at the library with the children?*
4. *We need a gift for your father.*
5. *My husband is in/at the library often with our children.*
6. *We never go to the mall without our* (female) *friends/girlfriends.*
7. *My sons are buying their/her mother a gift today.*
8. *My brother and his children are going to the mall.*
9. *My wife likes to go to the cinema with our children, but I do not like the cinema.*
10. *Are they helping me today?*

LESSON 130

1. *The dog is on the chair.*
2. *The dog is going onto the chair.*
3. *The chair is on the table.*
4. *Are her/their books on our table?*
5. *I do not have the newspaper. It is on the chair.*
6. *Y'all are in/at the school.*
7. *Her/Their mother and my father are in/at the supermarket.*
8. *My friends* (male or of mixed gender) *never go to the cinema without money.*
9. *My sister often goes to the library, but we never read books.*
10. *I never speak German with you, but you always speak German with me.*

LESSON 131

1. *I want a dog.*
2. *My sons want a cat.*
3. *Our brother wants my money, but I do not have money.*
4. *Does your mother want my car?*
5. *My sister wants ten dollars.*
6. *The dogs want food.*
7. *We want a car, but we do not need a car.*
8. *Our daughter needs a car, but she does not want a car.*
9. *The boys never go to the cinema without their friends* (male or of mixed gender).
10. *They like you, but do they like me?*

LESSON 132

1. to wash
2. to play
3. This sentence does not contain an infinitive.
4. to be
5. to forgive
6. to return
7. to play
8. This sentence does not contain an infinitive.
9. to buy
10. This sentence does not contain an infinitive.

LESSON 133

1. *I want to buy a book now.*
2. *Do you want to buy a car?*
3. *My sister wants to buy a newspaper.*
4. *We want to buy food, but we do not have money.*
5. *Do y'all want to buy a table?*
6. *They want to buy chairs and a table.*
7. *The newspaper is always on the table.*
8. *The cat often goes onto the chair.*
9. *My brother is in/at the park every day.*
10. *The boys like to go to the park with their/her dogs.*

LESSON 135

1. *I can go to the mall, but we cannot go to the supermarket.*
2. *My dogs cannot go to the library.*
3. *Your sister wants to go to the mall, but she cannot go.*
4. *The cat is always on the table.*
5. *Her/Their dog cannot go to the park.*
6. *We can go to school.*
7. *The cat likes to go onto the table.*
8. *The girls want to go to the mall, but we do not have money.*
9. *My daughters never go to the supermarket without their money.*
10. *My parents are in/at the school.*

LESSON 137

1. *You are.* OR *Y'all are.* OR *They are.*
2. *You are Mr. Johnson.*
3. *Are you Mrs. Smith?*
4. *Do you have a dog?* OR *Do y'all have a dog?*
5. *Do they have a dog?*
6. *Do you have a dog, Mrs./Miss/Ms. Jones?*
7. *Does she have a dog?*
8. *Where is the newspaper?*
9. *The newspaper? It is on the chair.*
10. *Do you/y'all go to the supermarket often?*

LESSON 138

1. *Are you going to the mall with your wife?*
2. *Mr. Smith, do you have your car?*
3. *Mrs. and Mr. Jones, are y'all buying a gift for y'all's children?*
4. *Mr. Johnson, do you want to talk about your cats?*
5. *Mrs./Miss/Ms. Smith, you never go to the mall without your money.*
6. *Mr. Underwood, do you speak German with your brother?*
7. *Mrs. and Mr. Smith, do y'all's parents go to the park every day?*
8. *Mrs./Miss/Ms. Johnson, I go to the cinema with your sister every week.*
9. *Mrs./Miss/Ms. Underwood, do you need food?*
10. *Mr. Smith, can you help me? Where is my brother?*

LESSON 141

1. *I like the woman's car.*
2. *The women's dogs are in/at the park.*
3. *We want to buy a gift for the woman's father, but we do not have money.*
4. *Do you see the woman's dog every week?*
5. *My son is speaking with the woman's daughter.*
6. *We like the men's cars.*
7. *My brother wants to buy the woman's car, but he has no money.*
8. *I like the woman's sister, but I don't like the woman's brother.*
9. *Where is the food? Do you/y'all have the cat's food?*
10. *Y'all do not have the men's money.*

LESSON 142

1. *The man's book is in/at the library.*
2. *We have the girl's dog.*
3. *I like the man's cat.*
4. *My daughter wants the woman's dog.*
5. *The boy is talking to the man's daughter.*
6. *We have the girls' gifts.*
7. *We do not have the supermarket's money.*
8. *She is not buying the man's phone.*
9. *The girl's father is my brother.*

10. *The man's son always wants to read books.*

LESSON 143

1. *Arnold's son seldom goes to the cinema.*
2. *Yes, Mrs./Miss/Ms. Jones's sister never goes to the park.*
3. *Bob's cat is on the chair.*
4. *My brother wants to buy Mr. Smith's car.*
5. *Mrs./Miss/Ms. Johnson, do you have Mrs./Miss/Ms. Smith's books?*
6. *He wants to talk about Mr. Johnson's children.*
7. *Mr. Smith's wife seldom goes to the mall without her* (female) *friends.*
8. *Do Fred's sons like cars?*
9. *Does Mr. Smith's sister speak German?*
10. *Do you want to buy a gift for Mr. Johnson's father?*

LESSON 144

1. *My brother's sons are in the park.*
2. *Our parents' cat is on the table.*
3. *My sister's money is on the table.*
4. *My mother's book is on the table.*
5. *Your father's newspaper is on the chair.*
6. *He likes my brother's car.*
7. *She often buys a gift for my* (male) *friend's/boyfriend's son.*
8. *Y'all's sister's phone is not on the table.*
9. *My brother's daughter is always reading books.*
10. *He has my brother's money.*

PRONUNCIATION GUIDE

This abbreviated guide to German pronunciation provides a few of the most important points to keep in mind when pronouncing German words.

CONSONANTS

j sounds like the *y* in *yoga*

s sounds like the *z* in *zebra* when it comes before a vowel. In other positions, it will have a hissing *s* sound as in English.

v sounds like the *f* in *father*

w sounds like the *v* in *violin*

z sounds like the *ts* in *hits*

ß sounds like the *ss* in *pass*

CONSONANT COMBINATIONS

ch sounds like the *h* in *huge* or like the *ch* in *Bach*

VOWELS

ä sounds like the *e* in *elephant*

ö sounds like the *e* in *bed*, but with rounded lips

ü sounds like the *e* in *feet*, but with rounded lips

VOWEL COMBINATIONS

ei sounds like the *i* in *fine*

eu sounds like the *oi* in *oil*

ie sounds like the *ee* in *queen*

GLOSSARY

aber *but*
Abend *evening*
acht *eight*
auch *also, too*
auf *on top of/onto*
auf Wiedersehen *see you later*
Auto *car*
Bibliothek *library*
bin *am*
bist *are*
brauchen *to need*
Bruder *brother*
Buch *book*
das *the*
dein *your*
der *the*
dich *you*
die *the*
dir *to you, for you*
drei *three*
du *you*
Durst *thirst*
ein *a, an*
eine *a, an*
Einkaufszentrum *mall, shopping center*
eins *one*
elf *eleven*
Eltern *parents*
er *he, it*
es *it*
Essen *food*
euer *y'all's*
Frau *woman, wife, Mrs., Miss, Ms.*
Freund *male friend, boyfriend*
Freundin *female friend, girlfriend*

fünf *five*
für *for*
Futter *food* (for animals)
geben *to give*
gehen *to go*
Geld *money*
gern/gerne *gladly*
Geschenk *gift*
guten Tag *good day, hello*
haben *to have*
Handy *mobile phone*
helfen *to help*
Herr *Mister*
heute *today*
Hund *dog*
Hunger *hunger*
ich *I*
ihr *y'all, her, their*
Ihr *your*
immer *always*
in *to, in, at*
ist *is*
ja *yes*
jede Woche *every week*
jeden Tag *every day*
jetzt *now*
Junge *boy*
Katze *cat*
kaufen *to buy*
kein *no*
Kind *child*
Kino *movie theater*
können *to be able*
lesen *to read*
Mädchen *girl*
Mann *man, husband*
mein *my*
mich *me*

mir *to me, for me*
mit *with*
mögen *to like*
Morgen *morning*
Mutter *mother*
Nacht *night*
nein *no*
neun *nine*
nicht *not*
nie *never*
null *zero*
oft *often*
ohne *without*
Park *park*
Schwester *sister*
sechs *six*
seid *are*
sein *his, its, to be*
selten *seldom*
sie *she, they, it*
Sie *you*
sieben *seven*
sind *are*
Sohn *son*
sprechen *to speak*
Stuhl *chair*
Tisch *table*
Tochter *daughter*
über *about*
und *and*
unser *our*
Vater *father*
vier *four*
Wasser *water*
wir *we*
wollen *to want*
zehn *ten*
Zeitung *newspaper*
zwei *two*
zwölf *twelve*